SUSTAINING NONPROFIT PERFORMANCE

CENTER
for **PUBLIC**
SERVICE

The Brookings Institution established the Center for Public Service in 1999 to answer three simple questions: what is the state of the public service today, how can the public sector issue a more compelling invitation to serve, and how can the public sector be a wise steward of the talent it recruits? The Center for Public Service espouses the simple belief that effective governance is impossible if public agencies, be they government or nonprofit, cannot compete for their fair share of talent in an increasingly tight labor market. Interested in more than basic research, the center aims to develop and disseminate pragmatic ideas that, if put to the test, will improve the odds that more talented Americans will enter the public service.

As part of this effort, the Center for Public Service has set forth an aggressive agenda to include a series of publications and reports, conferences, and other public events in order to encourage young Americans to enter the public service and to instill in all Americans a greater sense of confidence and integrity in that service. As with all Brookings publications, the judgments, conclusions, and recommendations presented in the studies are solely those of the authors and should not be attributed to the trustees, officers, or other staff members of the institution.

SUSTAINING NONPROFIT PERFORMANCE

The Case for Capacity Building and the Evidence to Support It

Paul C. Light

BROOKINGS INSTITUTION PRESS
Washington, D.C.

Copyright © 2004
THE BROOKINGS INSTITUTION
1775 Massachusetts Avenue, N.W., Washington, D.C. 20036
www.brookings.edu

Library of Congress Cataloging-in-Publication data

Light, Paul Charles.
Sustaining nonprofit performance : the case for capacity building and the
evidence to support it / Paul C. Light.
    p.   cm.
Includes bibliographical references and index.
ISBN 0-8157-5226-1 (cloth : alk. paper) —
ISBN 0-8157-5225-3 (pbk. : alk. paper)
    1. Nonprofit organizations—United States—Management. 2. Organizational
effectiveness. I. Title.

HD62.6.L545 2004
658.4'01—dc22   2004012674

9 8 7 6 5 4 3 2 1

The paper used in this publication meets minimum requirements of the American
National Standard for Information Sciences—Permanence of Paper for
Printed Library Materials: ANSI Z39.48-1992.

Typeset in Sabon with Myriad display

Composition by Cynthia Stock
Silver Spring, Maryland

Printed by R. R. Donnelley
Harrisonburg, Virginia

Contents

Preface

Sustaining Nonprofit Performance is the third of a series of volumes published as part of Brookings's Nonprofit Effectiveness Project, which was launched in 2000 with *Making Nonprofits Work*. That work examined the deluge of reform moving through the nonprofit sector and was followed by *Pathways to Nonprofit Excellence in 2002,* which looked at the characteristics of high-performing nonprofits. The project has also produced a series of policy briefs and short reports on public confidence in the nonprofit sector and the state of the nonprofit work force.

Nonprofits have been buffeted by many of the same questions about accountability and stewardship that rocked the private sector over the past three years. Whereas many of the private business scandals involved little more than greed, I argue that the nonprofit sector suffers from a different scandal—persistent underinvestment in its basic organizational infrastructure. Driven to do more with less, many nonprofits simply make do with the bare minimum, often denying their employees the training, technologies, and support they need to do their jobs.

This book draws primarily on a national survey of how the nonprofit sector has been responding to the increased pressure to perform. The case for capacity building is built by testing a series of simple logic chains that link capacity building to organizational performance and public confidence, and exploring the links through both careful statistical analysis and case studies of high-performing nonprofits conducted over the past two years. Although I argue that nonprofits can improve and sustain high performance through relatively low-cost, high-yield investments in their organizational infrastructure, a cautionary tale is offered here regarding how nonprofits can use their scarce resources wisely. Nonprofits cannot improve by merely throwing money at the latest management fad. Rather, they must think carefully about where they need to improve and what they want to accomplish.

This volume could not have written without the support of the David and Lucile Packard Foundation, which provided the funding for the national survey, the Robert Wood Johnson Foundation, which supported an early report on capacity building strategies, and the Carnegie Corporation of New York, which supported research toward a preliminary statement of the case for capacity building.

I am pleased to acknowledge my colleagues at Brookings, New York University, Princeton Survey Research Associates, and Third Sector New England, which publishes the *Nonprofit Quarterly*. In particular, I would like to acknowledge the help of Elizabeth Hubbard and Lisa Zellmer, who helped with the site visits to high-performing nonprofits, Ruth McCambridge and Cynthia Gibson, who helped with the preliminary statement, Mary McIntosh and her team at Princeton Survey Research Associates, who conducted the surveys referenced in the book, Ellen Schall and the rest of the intellectual community at the Robert F. Wagner School of Public Service at New York University, and Carol Graham, director of Governance Studies at the Brookings Institution.

Finally, I would like to thank the nonprofit employees and organizations that participated in the surveys and site visits, without whom this book could not have been written.

SUSTAINING NONPROFIT PERFORMANCE

1

The Pressure to Perform

These are times that try the nonprofit soul. Hardly a day goes by without a news story about a nonprofit or philanthropic foundation gone wrong. Congress seems ready to put strict limits on how much nonprofits can spend on administration and fund-raising. State attorneys general continue to grind through a seemingly endless list of investigations. A deeply divided nonprofit sector remains mostly silent in its own defense. Not surprising, perhaps, public confidence has hit a contemporary low.

Even as nonprofits face unrelenting scrutiny, the so-called jobless recovery has yet to produce a surge in charitable giving. Federal, state, and local governments are cutting discretionary spending wherever they can. Philanthropic investment strategies are becoming more conservative as the federal government's budget deficit grows and interest rates begin to climb. And individual giving remains sluggish. Not surprising, again, nonprofits are doing everything possible to access new revenues but are finding little investment capital available.

At the same time, the nation wants more of virtually everything that nonprofits deliver, but with no administrative costs. The baby boomers are starting to retire, creating a wave of board and staff vacancies and producing intense competition over the next generation of employees both inside the non-profit sector and against governments and private businesses. Nonprofit organizations are aging, too, with larger, older nonprofits becoming just as bureaucratic as the government agencies that fund them. To top it off, the nonprofit sector continues to add 3,000 to 4,000 new organizations every month, each one requiring at least some investment in organizational capacity, not to mention generating more competition for funding, staff, and board members.

The current crisis is unlike anything the nonprofit sector has ever faced. Watchdog groups are stronger and better staffed than ever. The media are better trained and more aggressive, too, and members of Congress and state officials are more engaged. The sector itself contains twice as many "targets" as it did just a decade ago, including the quasi-nonprofits created in the wake of campaign finance reform and the faith-based organizations that have emerged as potentially significant competitors for government support. In short, the past three years have created a "guilty-until-proven-innocent" climate that affects almost everything that matters to nonprofits: from raising money and managing volunteers to balancing the books and recruiting employees.

Defining the Crisis

Even a cursory sampling of guest editorials from the *Chronicle of Philanthropy* shows the range of opinion on addressing elements of this crisis. Claire Gaudiani argues for a "generosity revolution" built in part around a corporate tax credit designed to "enlarge the amount of money corporations learn to give and shareholders learn to accept as wise investments in the economy and society." Jeffrey Berry says nonprofits should stop hiding behind federal lobbying law as an "excuse for inaction," accept the fact that it is perfectly legal not only to lobby but to lobby extensively, and start giving "voice to those who can't speak for themselves." Lester Salamon urges the sector to confront the growing imbalance between "the nonprofit world's 'distinctiveness imperative,' that is, the things nonprofit groups do to remain distinct and thereby justify the special tax and other privileges they enjoy, and its 'survival imperative,' that is, the things these organizations must do to survive." William Schambra asks Congress to take on "big, elitist, bicoastal foundations" in search of a "more moderate, sober, humble philanthropy, no longer confident that it possesses a special capacity to shape public policy and more open to supporting citizen groups trying to design their own policies, however haltingly and unscientifically." Pablo Eisenberg urges Congress not to "squander its opportunity to clean up the nonprofit world," in part by increasing the Internal Revenue Service's enforcement budget by $250 million, of which at least $75 million would be earmarked for strengthening oversight by state attorneys general.[1]

Looking in the Mirror

There is much to embrace in these opinions and great hope that the sector's financial condition will improve once the recession ends, assuming that (1) the recession will ever end for nonprofits and that (2) private giving will somehow offset government cuts as budget deficits grow.[2] It is not clear, however, that increased funding, aggressive advocacy, and tougher enforcement will ease public worries about nonprofit performance.

More funding is unlikely to increase public confidence unless the sector can prove that nonprofits do a good job spending money wisely; more advocacy is unlikely to increase confidence unless the sector can make the case that nonprofits are doing a good job helping people, being fair in their decisions, and running their programs and services; and tougher oversight will not help unless the sector can address public concerns about nonprofit waste. Neither can the sector assert itself out of the current crisis by reminding Americans about all the good things it does. Many Americans no longer believe what the sector says on its own behalf, and few nationally recognized leaders are willing to stand up in its defense.

Absent strong objective evidence to the contrary and expanded investment in the organizational capacity to create it, public confidence is almost certain to continue its downward slide. According to an October 2003 telephone survey, only 14 percent of Americans said nonprofits did a very good job of spending money wisely, just 18 percent said the same about being fair in decisions, 21 percent about running programs and services, and 34 percent about helping people. As for stewardship, 60 percent of Americans said nonprofits wasted a great deal or a fair amount of money, while 46 percent said nonprofit leaders were paid too much, compared with just 8 percent who said they were paid too little.[3]

Bluntly put, Americans are not questioning *what* nonprofits do, but *how* nonprofits work. Asked to pick the largest problem facing the sector in October 2003, just 15 percent of Americans said nonprofits had the wrong programs for helping people, while 70 percent said nonprofits had the right programs but were simply inefficient. Put a different way, many Americans think the nonprofit sector has the right programs but that it often has the wrong organizations.

Discounting Reality

It is easy to discount these opinions as mere artifacts of negative press coverage. Yet, hard as it might be to accept, it is entirely possible that the public is more right than wrong about nonprofit performance. After all, millions of Americans are in the nonprofit sector every day, whether as donors, board members, employees, volunteers, or clients. In 2003 alone, roughly 100 million Americans volunteered, donated to, or worked in the nonprofit sector, and that does not include the millions more who went to the shelters, centers, theaters, museums, clinics, schools, marches, and campaigns organized by local organizations. If Americans can see the antiquated systems, executive pressure, employee burnout, constant scratching for dollars, leaky pipes, and broken windows, perhaps the nonprofit sector should see them, too.

Also hard as it might be to accept, former senator Bill Bradley (D-N.J.) and his McKinsey and Company colleagues could be right that the nonprofit sector has billions that it could put to better use through better management. "Imagine what an extra $100 billion a year could do for philanthropic and other nonprofit institutions," Bill Bradley, Paul Jansen, and Les Silverman write in the *Harvard Business Review*. "That's more than three times the annual giving of every charitable foundation in the United States. It's nearly twenty times the amount spent annually on Head Start. In fact, it's enough to give every high school graduate in the country a $40,000 scholarship."[4]

According to Bradley, Jansen, and Silverman, the vast majority of the sector's "$100 billion opportunity" resides in lowering the cost of raising and distributing funds, putting foundation assets to work faster, and improving the efficiency of program and administrative operations by "closing the gaps in performance between the more efficient nonprofits and the laggards." According to the estimates, benchmarking alone would help the bottom half of performers to reduce their service expenses 15 percent, which in turn would produce $55 billion that could be put to better use. Moreover, the savings would not stop there. "Our work with for-profits shows that even top performers can benefit from benchmarking individual functions because few organizations are at the peak level of performance across all of their activities. Thus any efficiency improvements among the top half of performers would further increase the savings.

The argument might be easier to accept if the estimates included the costs of implementation. It not only costs money to make money, it also costs money to save money. Equipping every nonprofit with the technology to raise funds on the Internet would cost billions, benchmarking would require both time and energy, not to mention occasional help from for-profit consulting firms such as McKinsey, strategic planning is both time-consuming and expensive, and McKinsey itself reports that mergers often underperform against expectations. Moreover, as Salamon argues in a scathing critique of the McKinsey analysis, "The McKinsey experts bring a combination of deep biases, serious misunderstandings, wild generalizations, half-truths, and sloppy reasoning to what charities need. In the process, they do a disservice to those who have dedicated their lives to improving the health and welfare of average Americans."[5]

As Salamon rightly argues, nonprofits are much better managed today than they were ten years ago. "This is no longer 'your grandfather's nonprofit sector' awaiting the arrival of the McKinsey geniuses to redeem it from sloth, but a resilient and competitive part of the American scene whose recent growth rate has exceeded that of the business world by 50 percent." Every survey I have conducted confirms Salamon's hunch about improvement: foundation executives believe it, as do scholars, consultants, and executive directors. And, as this book shows, nonprofits are doing a great deal to improve their performance every year.

However, as this book also shows, nonprofits are doing much of that work without any help. The vast majority of capacity building is self-funded and occurs with little or no contact with the outside world. Unlike the private sector, which spent more than $100 billion on consultants in 2003, nonprofits have little access to the kind of capital needed to update facilities and systems and often launch improvement efforts with limited planning and little objective data with which to measure success.

Thus, instead of arguing about where the McKinsey analysis is wrong, the nonprofit sector would be better off asking where it might be right. "We need to more deliberately create an expectation and demand among ourselves for measuring and improving our results on a regular basis," writes Alison Fine, director of a Washington-based evaluation firm called the Innovation Network. "We can continue squabbling among ourselves and allow others to prescribe what they think is best for us, weakening each other—and the sector—in the process. Or we can define the issues, frame the debate ourselves, and work collectively and with renewed vigor to establish what's truly important to our field, our organizations, and the people and communities we serve."[6]

Inside Opinions

If the nonprofit sector will not listen to the public or McKinsey, perhaps it will listen to Robert Egger, the sometimes caustic founder of the D.C. Central Kitchen and author of *Begging for Change*.[7] Some might discount the book for its dedication to punk rockers Joe Strummer and Joey Ramone, while others might wonder how a former nightclub owner found his way into nonprofit life. But none can doubt Egger's heart. He built the D.C. Central Kitchen from scratch as one of the first "food rescue" operations in the nation, took a brief leave of absence to help rescue the National Capital Area United Way from a Senate investigation, and remains one of the most visible figures in the antihunger movement.

More to the point of this book, Egger minces few words about the state of the nonprofit sector. Mega nonprofits such as the Salvation Army may have the dollars to invest in basic infrastructure, but most service agencies are constantly struggling to stay alive: "They struggle to hire and train employees. They're stuck between paying high salaries to their upper-level managers and offering respectable wages and benefits for lower-level employees. Many don't have the financial security to plan long-term goals. Some have to cobble together dozens and in some cases hundreds of different grants and subsidies to run their organizations, all of which have strings attached that in some way compromise the mission."

Egger overstates the level of nonprofit pay, which I believe significantly trails comparable government and private business jobs, and understates organizational mortality, which hovers well below government immortality, but above small-business turnover. However, I believe he is quite right about the sector's tolerance for bad behavior: "If our sector were subject to the same forces as the for-profit sector," he argues, "tens of thousands—maybe hundreds of thousands—of social service agencies would have merged, consolidated, or most likely gone out of business. Instead, they stay afloat because of lax IRS rules, an internal code of silence, and a public that hates to see an organization with a worthy cause go under, no matter how anemic it is."

Egger is also surely right about the need for further reform: "The only way to improve the nonprofit sector is for every constituency—the government, the private sector, the public, but most important, nonprofits themselves—to demand more and expect more from our nonprofits. We need to seek out and reward organizations that exemplify leadership, unity, responsibility, and accountability—and let go of those that can't or won't." He is also right about public confidence: "The recent downturn in public support for nonprofits isn't about the economy or 9/11. It's about skepticism. The public has had enough with pity and platitudes. Americans want a plan."

Those who do not believe this should talk to a nonprofit employee. As the next chapter shows, the nation's 12 million nonprofit employees are highly motivated, hard working, well led, and deeply committed, but they often serve in organizations that do not provide the resources they need to succeed. They are members of a first-rate work force often employed in second-rate organizations with third-rate equipment. Along with the chance to make miracles every day, nonprofit employees must tolerate high levels of stress and burnout, and many face persistent shortages of information, technology, training, and staff to do the job well. The nonprofit sector too often expects its work force to succeed in spite of organizational weaknesses that would collapse most businesses.

More to the point here, nonprofit employees have serious doubts about how their own organization works. Although they have much greater confidence in how their organization spends money, makes decisions, helps people, and runs programs and services than Americans in general, they report serious shortages in the basic resources needed both to achieve *and* to sustain high performance day after day. How can they sustain high performance when almost half say their organization only sometimes or rarely provides enough employees to do their job well? How can they sustain it when half describe their organization's hiring process as slow, or when a majority rate the quality of frontline employees as somewhat competent or less, and almost as many say the same of their board? How can they sustain it when 70 percent strongly or somewhat agree that it is easy to burn out in their job and that they always have too much work to do?

At least for now, the nonprofit sector survives because it has a self-exploiting work force: wind it up and it will do more with less until it just runs out. But at some point, the spring must break. As such, the current crisis is not at all about nonprofit hearts. Rather, it is about persistent organizational weaknesses that lead to the kinds of stories that invite public disquiet, media inquiry, congressional investigations, and demands for further regulation. Absent investments in nonprofit capacity, and the demonstrable gains in performance that such investments produce, the doubts will remain.

Plan of the Book

The challenge is to make a case for organizational investment at a time when nonprofits have little discretionary funding and must often choose between computers and kids, training and trees, salaries and seniors. Absent strong empirical evidence that capacity building actually produces the promised increase in capacity, which in turn produces the hoped-for increase in effectiveness, nonprofits pick the kids, trees, and seniors every time.

Chapter 2 provides the basic logic for this book by linking organizational capacity to discretionary giving and volunteering. The chapter starts by examining the nonprofit sector's capacity deficit and then argues that capacity affects organizational effectiveness, which shapes public confidence, which affects the willingness to contribute money and time to nonprofits other than one's own religious institution or alma mater. Although the statistical case is built on perceptions of capacity and effectiveness, the linkages between these key predictors of organizational performance are strong and clear nonetheless.

Chapter 3 examines the current state of capacity building by asking what nonprofits have done lately to improve organizational effectiveness. After examining the meager evidence on whether capacity building works, the chapter introduces the national survey of nonprofits that underpins the book. The chapter examines the recent history of organizational improvement among the 318 nonprofits that participated in the study. Although these nonprofits have been working hard to improve their organizational performance, the chapter shows that they have been doing at least some of that work without the full engagement of their boards and frontline staff and without adequate planning, funding, external contact, and objective measurement.

Chapter 4 takes the case for capacity building further by asking whether and how these improvement efforts changed the organizations in which they occurred. Simply asked, if capacity is important to effectiveness, does capacity building actually improve capacity? The chapter starts with basic questions about how to measure success in the absence of a hard bottom line against which to compare organizations before and after an improvement effort. It then examines a basket of possible measures that might be used as surrogates of success and proceeds to an analysis of why some of the efforts are judged as more successful than others. As the chapter concludes, it does not matter where the funding comes from, but it must be adequate.

Chapter 5 offers a brief inventory of advice for nonprofits on how to improve the odds of capacity-building success. Regardless of their age, size, or state of their budget, nonprofits that use evidence to track their capacity-building efforts, make more contact with the outside world, raise even a small amount of funding for their effort, and do advance planning are always more successful than their peers. The value of outside contact depends, in part, on the strength of the nonprofit infrastructure. It hardly makes sense to call on the consulting community, read a book or manual, or attend a training workshop if the consultants are weak, the books are dense, and the training is overpriced. The chapter concludes with a brief discussion of the urgent need to recruit the next generation of nonprofit employees. The sector is in a war for talent in a shrinking labor market but does not seem to know it.

Chapter 6 concludes the book by asking how nonprofits actually use capacity building to advance up a spiral of nonprofit excellence. Drawing on twenty-five case studies of high-performing nonprofits in Atlanta, Chicago, Indianapolis, Los Angeles, Minneapolis, New York City, San Diego, San Francisco, and Washington, the chapter argues that nonprofits move up and down a spiral that begins with organic questions about how the organization will make a difference, who does what, why it exists, and how it will know it is successful, if it is, and ends with reflective questions about legacy and renewal. As the chapter argues, there is nothing automatic about movement up the spiral—nonprofits move up and down the spiral as they confront crises and shocks, new opportunities and problems, leadership and board transitions, and the natural problems of growth and decline.

This is a research report, not a how-to book. It builds the case for organizational investment on hard evidence, not anecdote, and is based on five years and $2 million of data, including four major sources: (1) a 2001 random-sample survey of 1,140 nonprofit employees, (2) a 2003 random-sample survey of 770 Americans, (3) a 2003 random-sample survey of 318 nonprofits with annual budgets at or above $25,000, and (4) twenty-five case studies of high-performing nonprofits in the nine cities noted above. The book also draws on past surveys by the Center for Public Service of employees in federal government, business, and low-income-serving children, youth, and family agencies, a string of public opinion surveys on confidence in nonprofits, and my two earlier book-length studies of nonprofit effectiveness.[8] Much of this work was supported by the David and Lucile Packard Foundation, including the national survey of nonprofit capacity building that forms the backbone of this book.

Although many nonprofit executives and employees accept the case for capacity building, their donors and boards often underestimate the need for capacity building during hard times. Moreover, I have heard more than a few nonprofit executives describe technology, training, strategic planning, and so forth as luxuries of a kind. My hope is that a healthy blast of evidence will convince donors, boards, and even a few executive directors that building capacity is very much a necessity for sustainable effectiveness. Although at times the book may overwhelm readers with percentages, I believe it is time for a good old-fashioned overwhelming.

Conclusions

Some readers will argue that restoring public confidence is a slender rationale for investing in organizational capacity. Public opinion is notoriously unstable and easily influenced by the latest scandal, yet hard to change once it turns negative. Moreover, if Americans have not noticed the reengineering and reinventing that Salamon celebrates, how can anyone expect them to notice a new wave of capacity building?

A first answer is that confidence is both a leading and a lagging indicator of the changing market for scandal. Its decline creates a political market for negative coverage by the media, Congress, state attorneys general, and watchdog groups, which in turn creates further erosion. Just as declining trust in government has created a market for bureaucrat bashing and an unrelenting campaign against Washington and waste, declining confidence in nonprofits has created a climate for nonprofit bashing. It is a vicious cycle well worth stopping early.

The second answer is that declining confidence is a signpost of changing donor and volunteer attitudes. Donors and volunteers are demanding greater returns on their "investments" as their worries grow about nonprofit performance. Although one cannot say for sure that giving and volunteering will decline in absolute dollars and hours if confidence does not rebound, expectations most certainly have and will change. The donor choice movement began well before September 11, for example, but has accelerated since, in part because leading nonprofits such as the American Red Cross have been pressed to guarantee 100 percent pass-through on disaster relief.

A third answer is that confidence is a perfectly valid measure of organizational effectiveness, both for the sector as a whole and for individual nonprofits such as the Red Cross and United Way. Used in a basket of indicators that covers program and financial outcomes, confidence does reveal something about an organization's impact on its world. As we see shortly, public confidence in the Red Cross and United Way have improved over the past year due in large part to board development, new leadership, media relations, and strategic planning, all of which are forms of organizational capacity building. Although the gains have not affected confidence in the sector as a whole, they show that confidence can and does respond to organizational improvement.

Confidence is also an often-overlooked measure of regulatory outcomes, whether for the Internal Revenue Service, Congress, state attorneys general, inspectors general, or watchdog groups. In theory, increased regulatory activity should produce overall gains in nonprofit performance, whether through audits of individual nonprofits, adoption of best practices, or creation of what a federal inspector general has described as the "visible odium of deterrence."[9] In practice, however, most watchdogs prefer to be measured by their bite, meaning the number of audits and investigations opened, dollars recovered, indictments, and funds put to better use, rather than by public confidence. Nevertheless, it seems reasonable to hold watchdogs to some higher standard.

Finally, confidence clearly has some bearing on employee productivity and pride. At least in 2001, the vast majority of nonprofit employees said they felt proud to tell their friends and neighbors what they did for a living, and just under half said they were very satisfied with the public respect they received from their work. At least in 2001, nonprofit employees were also far more likely to trust their own organization to do the right thing than either federal government or business employees. But even in 2001, there were warning signs about the future: nearly a third of the nonprofit employees interviewed said that, all things considered, they would rather work in government or business, and half said they would receive the same amount of respect in a job outside the sector.

Unfortunately, there are no comparable trend data showing the corrosive effects on employee attitudes of declining confidence in the federal government. But there was a time when the public trusted the government to do the right thing, thought salaries were reasonable, perceived waste to be low, and trusted most agencies to spend money wisely, make fair decisions, help people, and run their programs and services efficiently. The nonprofit sector may well be at a similar moment today. Absent investment and self-regulation, the sector may someday soon find itself longing for the golden days when only 60 percent of Americans thought nonprofits wasted a great deal or a fair amount of money and when 14 percent thought nonprofits did a very good job spending money wisely.

I also believe that organizational investment is warranted even if improved effectiveness has no impact whatsoever on confidence. Indeed, the key link in the case for capacity building is not between organizational effectiveness and public confidence, but between organizational capacity and effectiveness. As this book shows, relatively small investments in capacity building can improve organizational capacity, which, in turn, can produce significant gains in output such as staff morale, management focus, public reputation, efficiency, and productivity, which, in turn, can produce significant gains in perceived management and program effectiveness. If those gains in organizational effectiveness produce gains in public confidence, all the better. But the case for capacity building is well made on the basis of organizational effectiveness alone.

2 | The Logic of Investment

This book starts from the premise that nonprofits make miracles every day. Name a difficult national or international problem since World War II, and the nonprofit sector has played a role in addressing it, whether through its research, innovation, entrepreneurial spirit, or advocacy.

Consider the government's greatest achievements of the past half century, which were identified in a survey of 450 leading historians and political scientists.[1] Nonprofit advocacy was essential to the success of the civil rights movement, for example, which produced three of the federal government's top five achievements: expanding the right to vote (number two), ending discrimination in public accommodations (number three), and reducing workplace discrimination (number five). Nonprofit research was central to the battle against life-threatening diseases such as polio and tuberculosis (number four), the campaigns to improve food safety and protect water (number six) and to restore clean air and water (numbers eleven and fifteen), and the battle to balance the federal budget (number nine). Its voice was essential to improving health care and financial security for older Americans (numbers eight and ten), and its intellectual energy helped to create support for rebuilding Europe after World War II (number one).

13

Equally important, the nonprofit sector was essential in filling the gaps created by government's greatest disappointments. It continues to provide the basic services and energy behind renewing poor communities (number four on the list of failures), increasing the supply of low-income housing (number six), expanding job training (number seven), helping the working poor (number ten), advancing humanitarian rights abroad (number thirteen), and improving elementary and secondary education (number fifteen).

The question is not whether nonprofits make miracles every day, but whether they need more organizational help to do so. At least according to their employees, the answer is emphatically yes. Nonprofits have been doing more with less for so long that many now border on doing everything with nothing. Forced to cut something, nonprofits target organization and management almost every time, even if it means another year with leaky pipes and broken windows. And who is to say they are wrong? Again, absent strong evidence to the contrary, nonprofits always serve their mission first, even if doing so creates high stress and turnover.[2]

This chapter provides strong evidence, based on employee and public perceptions, for a contrary view. As figure 2-1 shows, the logic of organizational investment depends on a simple chain that runs from organizational capacity all the way through discretionary giving and volunteering.

The first link in the chain is supported by evidence collected through a 2001 random-sample telephone survey of nonprofit employees. According to the survey, nonprofit employees who said they always or often had access to organizational resources such as information, training, enough staff, and technology were more likely than their less well-supported peers to say their organization did a very or a somewhat good job running programs and services, spending money wisely, being fair in decisions, and helping people. In turn, nonprofit employees who said their organization did a very or a somewhat good job at these tasks were also more likely than their less enthusiastic peers to say they trusted their organization to do the right thing just about always or most of the time.

The second and third links in the chain are supported by evidence collected through a 2003 random-sample telephone survey of the American public. According to the survey, Americans who said nonprofits did a very or a somewhat good job running programs and services, spending money wisely, being fair in decisions, and helping people were more likely than their less enthusiastic peers to say they had a great deal or a

FIGURE 2-1. The Logic of Organizational Effectiveness

fair amount of confidence in nonprofits in general. In turn, Americans who said they had a great deal or a fair amount of confidence were also more likely than their less confident peers to say they had given money or time to nonprofits other than their religious institution or alma mater.

Although both patterns clearly reinforce the linkages outlined in figure 2-1, the links are based on perceptions—and perceptions alone. Given the lack of objective data for measuring nonprofit capacity and effectiveness, perceptions will have to do for now. Although perceptions are always affected by self-interest, the evidence presented here is strong enough to make the case that capacity matters to the effectiveness of nonprofit organizations, which is more than enough to justify further analysis of whether and how capacity-building efforts work.

The Shortage of Nonprofit Capacity

Organizational capacity encompasses virtually everything an organization uses to achieve its mission, from desks and chairs to programs and people. Measured at any given point in time, capacity is an output of basic organizational activities such as raising money, forging partnerships, organizing work, recruiting and training board members, leaders, and employees, generating ideas, managing budgets, and evaluating programs. Once created, organizational capacity is consumed in mission-related program activities such as treating patients, feeding the hungry, building housing, producing art, educating students, training workers, and so forth. Once expended, it is regenerated through the same organizational activities that created it in the first place.

Viewed as an input to program impact, the case for capacity building starts with the need for more capacity. It could be that nonprofits are generating and regenerating enough organizational capacity to succeed.

It could be that they have done more than enough restructuring, reengineering, planning, partnering, collaborating, streamlining, communicating, designing, recruiting, and training to become exemplars of perpetual motion. If so, additional capacity building would be a waste of time, not to mention a distraction from the mission and a potential breach of fiduciary responsibility.

Unfortunately, there is ample evidence that the nonprofit sector consumes more capacity each day than it actually has—hence the high levels of employee burnout and stress. According to my surveys of federal government, business, and nonprofit employees, the nonprofit sector has considerable strengths, not the least of which is being the most motivated work force in the nation, if not the world. At the same time, the surveys show persistent organizational weaknesses that reveal the need for additional organizational investment.[3]

Assets

Start with the assets. According to head-to-head comparisons across the three sectors, nonprofit workers are the most motivated employees in the economy. They take their job for the right reasons and come to work each day motivated by the right goals. Asked why they took their current job, nonprofit employees were much more likely to say that they took their job for the chance to help the public, *not* for the security, to make a difference, *not* for the salary and benefits, and to help people, *not* for a secure paycheck. And they take pride in the organization. Asked why they came to work each day, nonprofit employees were twice as likely as federal and business employees to focus on the nature of the job and the common good and half as likely to focus on the compensation and work ethic.

Nonprofit employees also see their own organization as a better place to work. They were more likely than federal or business employees to say their colleagues were open to new ideas, willing to help other employees learn new skills, and concerned about achieving their organization's mission. They were also more likely than federal and business employees to describe their organization as helpful, fair, and trusted and were just a few percentage points behind the business employees in describing their organization as innovative.

Finally, nonprofit employees have the greatest clarity about their job. They were the most likely to say that they could easily describe their organization's mission and the most likely to say that they contributed a great deal to accomplishing that mission. They were also the least likely to describe their work as boring and their job as a dead end with no future. They were also more likely than federal and business employees to describe employee morale as very high and to rate their organization's leadership, middle-level employees, and lower-level employees as competent and improving quickly. They were more proud than other employees to tell their friends and neighbors where they worked, more likely to trust their organization to do the right thing, and the most likely to say that their organization did a very good job at running programs and services, spending money wisely, being fair in decisions, and helping people.

Deficit

Unfortunately, nonprofit employees often succeed in spite of persistent underinvestment in other forms of organizational capacity. Nonprofit employees were less likely than business employees to report that their organization provided enough information, technological equipment, employees, and training to do their job well and rarely trailed federal employees on these key resources by more than a few percentage points. They were also more likely than their federal and business peers to say that the poor performers in their organization were failing because they did not have the training to do their job and equally likely to say that poor performers were simply not qualified for their job. Asked specifically about working conditions, 70 percent agreed that they always had too much work to do, and 73 percent agreed that it was easy to burn out in their job.[4]

Nonprofit employees were much less likely than either federal or business employees to be very or somewhat satisfied with their salary and much more likely to believe that their salary and benefits would be better at another job outside a nonprofit organization. They were also just as likely as their federal and business peers to say that their organization was having problems recruiting and retaining talented employees at their level of the organization. They were just as likely as business employees to say that their organization did a poor job at disciplining poor performers.

The sector-by-sector comparisons clearly suggest substantial opportunities to strengthen nonprofit capacity. To paraphrase the Rolling Stones, nonprofit employees not only don't get the capacity they want, they often don't get what they need and certainly don't get what they deserve.

Moreover, even when their sector emerges on top in the comparisons, there are still troubling signs of organizational distress:

—Only a quarter of nonprofit employees said their organization did a great deal to encourage employees to take risks or to try new ways of doing their work.

—Two-fifths said the word "innovative" described their organization somewhat well, not too well, or not well at all.

—Only a fifth said overall morale was very high, compared with half who said it was somewhat high and a quarter who said it was somewhat low or very low.

—Nearly half said that more than 10 percent of their coworkers were not performing their job well, and roughly a third put the estimate at more than 20 percent.

—Three-fifths said the quality of their organization's board, executive director, middle-level employees, and lower-level employees had either remained the same or declined over the past five years.

—A quarter described their organization's hiring process as confusing, and half described it as slow.

—More than two-fifths said their organization either did not do too good a job or did not do a good job at all of disciplining poor performers.

—Only a fifth of the employees who said that their organization had been reformed or reinvented in recent years said the effort had made their job a lot easier, while almost a third said it had made their job somewhat or a lot more difficult.

—More than two-fifths said their organization only sometimes or rarely provided enough employees to do its job well.

—Less than half said they always trusted their organization to do the right thing.

These organizational frustrations are particularly noticeable in older nonprofits, where age often creates needless bureaucracy. Employees at older nonprofits were less likely to say that the people they worked with were open to new ideas or willing to help other employees learn new skills, for example, and were less likely to say that their organization encouraged employees to take risks and to try new ways of doing their work. They were also less likely to say that they could easily describe how their job contributed to the mission, to call their organization helpful, fair, and trusted, or to agree that they were given a chance to do the things they do best.

Age also has a formidable impact when combined with organizational size. Nonprofit employees in larger, older organizations see much more bureaucracy than their colleagues in smaller, younger organizations. And despite their reputation for having more resources to distribute, their employees are more likely to complain that they do not have access to enough employees to do the job. Thus employees in larger, older nonprofits were twice as likely as employees in smaller, younger organizations to describe their hiring process as confusing, more likely to describe it as slow, and more likely to say that their organization did not do a good job at disciplining poor performers.[5] They were less likely to report that their coworkers were open to new ideas, were willing to help other employees learn new skills, and were committed to the organization's mission, and they reported lower morale, higher stress, and lower quality at all levels of the organization. Most important, they also gave their organization lower ratings on spending money wisely, being fair, helping people, and running their programs and services. Thus 60 percent of employees in younger, smaller organizations said their organization did a very good job spending money wisely, compared to just 34 percent in older, larger organizations. Similarly, 60 percent in younger, smaller organizations also said their organization did a very good job being fair in their decisions, compared to just 36 percent in older, larger organizations.[6]

The Opportunity for Improvement

These statistics suggest plenty of room for strengthening nonprofit capacity. While 11 percent of nonprofit employees said their organization needed major reforms, only 23 percent said their organization did not need much reform at all.

The nonprofit sector has already done a great deal to move these sentiments in the right direction, however. Nonprofits are no doubt better managed today than they were ten years ago, in part because of the sector's "gusto" for reform, as Salamon calls it.[7] According to the survey, 60 percent of nonprofits had reformed or reinvented how they work in recent years, compared with 56 percent of businesses and 73 percent of federal government agencies.

More to the point of this book, much of the reform was successful. Asked how their organization's reform had affected them, 61 percent of nonprofit employees said it had made their job a lot or somewhat easier, compared with 60 percent of business employees but just 41 percent of federal employees. Although making jobs easier is not the primary aim of most reforms, the constant push for reform clearly has improved nonprofit life.

Nonprofit employees are willing to consider just about any idea for improving performance except one. When asked to think about the mission of their organization, only 7 percent said there were too many nonprofits performing the same mission, while 56 percent said there was the right number, and 32 percent said there were too few.

Otherwise, nonprofit employees saw gains from a host of recent reforms. When asked to think back over the past five years about all the reforms they had seen come and go, employees who had either worked in the sector for at least ten years or were managers at the time of the survey saw benefits in almost every type of reform that had come across the transom: 73 percent said strategic planning had achieved a great deal or a fair amount of impact in improving the performance of their organization, 73 percent said the same about increased openness to using standard business tools, 71 percent about the encouragement to collaborate, 68 percent about the increased emphasis on the measurement of outcomes, and 62 percent about the creation of management standards. In fact, the only reform that did not earn high praise was the effort to reduce duplication and overlap through mergers and alliances: only 42 percent said the reform had achieved a great deal or a fair amount of impact on their organization.

These employees did not think it was time to take a break, however. When asked to look forward and offer any ideas they thought might improve their organization, the respondents who said their own organization needed major repair offered a long list of ideas that can be grouped into four broad categories:

—64 percent of nonprofit employees said their organization needed to reduce bureaucracy, improve communication, and increase access to staff, training, technology, and funding. The category included a wide range of answers. One respondent said, "There is too much cream on top; we need to get rid of the weight up above." Another said, "People higher up need to come down to the lower level to experience the day-to-day work there." And a third recommended an effort to "streamline the basic work flow, get more innovation in frontline decisionmaking, and reduce multiple layers needed for approval."

—26 percent said their organization needed to reward a job well done. One respondent said, "We need a different level based on performance." Another urged the organization to "spend more time in training, teach responsibility, and show the effects of a job not getting done." And another recommended "more focus on employee satisfaction and a pat on the back when something good happens."

—16 percent focused on the need for a more talented, diverse, well-managed work force and more engaged boards. One said, "We need to attract more qualified people who will stay." Another recommended "a new board, new upper level management, and more employees at the middle level." And another said, "We need to do more than just talk about diversity; we need to actually do something about it."

—7 percent said their organization needed a clearer mission. One said, "We need to stop dreaming so big." Another recommended "walking the walk, talking the talk, living up to the mission." And another simply said, "Stay on track."

It is hard to find a single pattern in the answers except the desire for improvement. These seasoned employees clearly believe that nonprofits should keep improving, especially in removing the natural obstacles that emerge with age and growth.

The Link between Organizational Capacity and Effectiveness

Just because many nonprofit employees are stressed out and under-resourced does not mean that their organizations are somehow less effective in achieving results. Neither does it mean that more organizational capacity is the answer to every complaint.

Moreover, even strong supporters of capacity building are not always sure about the link between capacity and organizational effectiveness. As surveys of grant makers, consultants, and executive directors show, organizations can be very effective in achieving their mission and not be well managed, meaning that organizational effectiveness is not necessary for high performance. At the same time, organizations can be very well managed and still not achieve their mission, meaning that organizational effectiveness is not sufficient for program impacts.[8]

Yet poorly run organizations cannot produce program impacts for long, which may be why so many respondents recommended that poorly performing organizations should work first on becoming well managed rather than on improving their program design. Any organization, no matter how moribund and inefficient, can be effective for a time. All it needs are extraordinary employees who are willing to put up with old computers, stress, and burnout. The trick is both to achieve *and* to sustain the effectiveness over time. The only way I know of doing so is by building organizational capacity. Nonprofits can only produce miracles for so long without the infrastructure to do so. The challenge is to prove the link in statistical terms.

Rating Organizational Effectiveness

Unlike private businesses, where success is easily measured by profit and shareholder value, the nonprofit sector has few objective measures of programmatic effectiveness that might allow comparisons across organizations. The best we can do to test the link between organizational capacity and effectiveness is to ask employees to rate their own organization and then to ask whether the ratings are linked to measures of organizational capacity.

Nonprofit employees obviously have some self-interest in seeing their own organization and sector as better than they actually are. The 1,140 nonprofit employees surveyed in late 2001 were much more likely than their federal government and business peers to say that they took their current job for the chance to help people, make a difference, and do something worthwhile and because of their pride in the organization.

Nonprofit employees were also much more likely to say they came to work each day because of the nature of the job and their desire to contribute to the common good. Given the chance to give as many answers as they wished, nonprofit employees focused much more on the work itself:

—41 percent of nonprofit employees said they came to work for their personal interest in the job, because they liked their work, or for the spiritual rewards. This category included a variety of answers. For example, one respondent simply said, "I love what I do." Another said, "I love working with the clients." Another answered, "I understand and embrace the mission of the organization." And others responded, "I love my job, I love the kids, it's fun," "It's a wonderful match for my skills, background, and interest," and "I'm passionate about what I do."

—16 percent said they came to work for the paycheck. One answered, "I need a paycheck"; another, "I need the money"; and others, "It is a way to make a living," "I have five years to retirement," and "There's no one to pay the mortgage and bills."

—11 percent focused on their personal work ethic. One simply said, "That's my job." Another said, "I am a very dependable person." And another said, "I'm responsible, what can I say?"

—10 percent focused exclusively on the common good. One respondent answered, "I can make a difference." Another said, "I can make a difference, and that's where God wants me to be." And another said, "Whatever I accomplish is worthwhile and necessary."

Asked the same question, just 5 percent of federal employees and none of the business respondents said they came to work each day for the common good, while 31 percent of federal employees and 47 percent of private sector employees said they came to work every day solely for the paycheck.

Given their basic motivations for coming to work in the morning, it is no surprise that nonprofit employees also saw their sector as doing a very good job at running programs and services (56 percent), spending money wisely (44 percent), being fair (45 percent), or helping people (73 percent). There is always some self-interest in such rankings, although apparently less self-interest among federal government and business employees, who consistently rated their own sector lower on all four indicators.[9]

The bigger surprise is that government and business employees also rated the nonprofit sector as the best at helping people, while government employees rated it as the best at spending money wisely, and business employees rated it as the best at running programs. Whereas 32 percent of federal government employees said the federal government was the best at helping people, 42 percent said nonprofits were the best; and whereas 33 percent of business employees said for-profit businesses were the best at spending money wisely, 35 percent said nonprofits were the best.

Explaining Organizational Effectiveness

Even acknowledging self-interest, not all nonprofit employees see exceptional effectiveness in their midst: 25 percent said their organization did either somewhat good, not too good, or not good at all in helping people, 43 percent said the same about running programs and services, 52 percent said the same about spending money wisely, and 57 percent said the same about being fair in decisions. When these four measures are summed together into a general assessment of overall effectiveness, the survey of nonprofit employees provided more than enough variation against which to judge the relative consequence of organizational life.

The survey also contained a long list of possible explanations for the effectiveness each employee saw. Employees were asked to rate their organization as innovative, fair, helpful, and trusted; coworkers as cooperative, open to new ideas, willing to help each other, and committed to the mission; the hiring process as simple or confusing, fast or slow, fair or unfair; the level of access to information and training and the amount of employees and equipment as adequate or not; the impact of recent reforms in making jobs easier, cutting management layers, and reducing the need for further reform; the overall competence of the board, senior leadership, middle-level managers, middle-level employees, and lower-level employees; as well as their own pride and trust in the organization. As a group, these measures help to define organizational capacity much more precisely as the competencies, relationships, management systems, and resources that are consumed in day-to-day program activities.

The key question is whether these measures have any bearing on organizational effectiveness. Does access to technology improve the odds that nonprofits will spend money wisely or just create distraction? Do helpful coworkers improve the odds that nonprofits will be fair in decisions or just make the organization a friendlier place to work? Does a fast, simple hiring process improve the odds that nonprofits will help people or just enable higher turnover? Do competent leaders improve performance or simply make life easier?

The survey of nonprofit employees provided answers to some of these questions. Alongside all the questions about their job, the 1,140 nonprofit employees were also asked how well their organization did at running programs and services, spending money wisely, being fair in decisions, and helping people. Once these views are summed into a single, more robust measure of perceived performance, further statistical analysis can address both whether and how organizational capacity actually matters to perceived effectiveness.[10] Although it is not possible to test every measure of organizational capacity without jeopardizing the validity of the results, box 2-1 summarizes what emerged from the head-to-head statistical comparison of nineteen possible explanations of organizational effectiveness: (1) the respondent's level in the organization; (2) the respondent's sense of personal accomplishment; (3) the respondent's ability to describe mission of the organization; (4) the respondent's sense that his or her own job was a dead end with no future; (5) the respondent's sense that his or her own job provided the chance to do the things the respondent does best; the respondent's rating

---

BOX 2-1. Statistically Significant Explanations of Nonprofit Effectiveness

The following ten explanations of nonprofit effectiveness, which were based on a sample size of 1,140, are statistically significant:

1. Rating of the organization as innovative, helpful, fair, and trusted,
2. Pride in the organization,
3. Competence of executive director,
4. Rating of the disciplinary process,
5. Rating of past reform as having made the job easier to do, reducing the need for further reform, and producing fewer layers of management,
6. Access to information, training, enough staff, and technology,
7. Rating of the hiring process as fast and simple,
8. Competence of middle-level employees,
9. Competence of the board,
10. Being a senior staffer in the organization.

Note: These results were produced through ordinary least-squares regression of a summed measure of nonprofit effectiveness (running programs and services + spending money wisely + being fair + helping people) among employees in the 2001 survey. Strength is measured using standardized beta weights, and significance is based on t tests, which indicate the chance that a given result is not the result of random occurrence. The adjusted R^2 for the overall model is 0.605, which means that the analysis explains roughly 61 percent of the variation in employee views of overall effectiveness, which is significant at the 0.000 level. The list only includes explanations that are significant at the 0.05 level or greater, which means 95 percent confidence that the explanations are statistically significant predictors of organizational effectiveness.

---

of the competency of the organization's (6) board, (7) executive director, (8) middle-level employees, and (9) lower-level employees; (10) the respondent's rating of the organization's ability to attract top candidates for jobs at the respondent's level; (11) the respondent's rating of the hiring system as fast and simple; (12) the respondent's rating of the organization's ability to discipline poor performers; (13) a summed measure of the respondent's perceived access to information, training, enough employees, and technology; (14) the respondent's estimated percentage of coworkers not doing their job well; (15) a summed measure of the respondent's rating of coworkers as not competitive with each other, helpful, willing to try new things, and committed to the organizational mission; (16) a summed rating of the respondent's rating of past organizational reforms in making jobs easier to do, reducing the need for further reform, and producing fewer layers between the top and bottom of the organization; (17) the respondent's rating of his or her personal contribution to the organizational mission; (18) the respondent's pride in the organization; and (19) the respondent's rating of the organization as innovative, trusted, helpful, and fair.

As box 2-1 shows, ten of the eighteen measures are significant predictors of effectiveness. Organizational capacity clearly matters to employee perceptions of overall effectiveness. Creating an overall culture of innovation, trust, fairness, and helpfulness is the most powerful explanation for effectiveness, followed by instilling pride in the organization (which may be more a consequence than a cause of perceived effectiveness), recruiting a competent board and senior staff, and building an effective disciplinary process.

While acknowledging that being a senior employee creates self-interest in seeing one's own organization as well performing, organizational basics are critically important levers for increasing perceived effectiveness. So are reforms that make jobs easier to do, reduce the distance between the top and bottom of the organization, and eliminate the need for major reform in the future. To the extent one accepts the premise that employee perceptions of performance are closely related to reality, this analysis lends significant support to those who believe in the utility of board and staff training, team building, strategic planning, new technologies, participatory management, and a host of other approaches for improving organizational life.

What the analysis cannot show is whether an organization's mission and programs are themselves a source of perceived effectiveness. Simply put, *what* an organization does through its programs and services may be just as important in shaping effectiveness as *how* the organization operates. Employees can hardly accomplish something worthwhile if their mission is impossible, for example, and they cannot be helpful to each other if their programs are unworkable. My hunch is that employees think about programs and services when they answer questions about accomplishing something worthwhile in their job, trusting their organization to do the right thing, and believing that they contribute to the mission of their agency, but this is only a hunch.

TABLE 2-1. **Statistically Significant Explanations for Nonprofit Effectiveness, by Sector**[a]

Ranking by employees of the sector

Explanation	Nonprofits	Federal government	Private businesses
Rating the organization as innovative, helpful, fair, and trusted	1	1	2
Taking pride in the organization	2	4	4
Competence of the executive director or senior leadership	3	2	n.s.
Rating of the disciplinary process	4	n.s.	n.s.
Rating of past reform as having made the job easier to do reducing the need for further reform and producing fewer layers of management	5	7	1
Access to information, training, enough staff, and technology	6	5	3
Rating of the hiring process as fast and simple	7	n.s	n.s.
Competence of middle-level employees	8	6	n.s.
Competence of the board	9	n.a.	n.a.
Being a senior staffer in the organization	10	n.s.	n.s.
Believing the organization does a good job attracting top candidates for jobs	n.s.	3	5
Rating of coworkers as not competitive, willing to try new things, helpful, and committed	n.s.	8	n.s.
Sample size	1,140	1,051	1,005

Source: Surveys conducted by Princeton Survey Research Associates on behalf of the Center for Public Service.
n.s. Not significant.
n.a. Question not asked of sample.
a. All three analyses explain a very high percentage of variation in employee perceptions of overall effectiveness. The adjusted R^2 is 0.618 for the nonprofit analysis, 0.618 for the federal analysis, and 0.665 for the business analysis. All three are significant at the 0.000 level.

As table 2-1 shows, the explanations for effectiveness vary greatly across the three sectors. Although coworkers and trust are statistically significant explanations in all three sectors, the disciplinary process is only significant among nonprofit employees, but not among their federal or private peers; the recruitment process is significant for federal and private employees, but not for nonprofit employees; and having adequate access to resources is important for nonprofit and private employees, but not for their federal peers.

The results do not prove that disciplinary systems or middle-level employees are somehow irrelevant to federal or business performance or that recruiting talented workers is irrelevant to nonprofits. Rather, they suggest that the initial motivations for taking a job are more important for explaining performance in the nonprofit sector and the federal government than in the private sector, while the quality of middle-level employees may vary somewhat more in the nonprofit sector and, therefore, may play a greater role in explaining performance. As such, the rankings are best viewed as a rough inventory of what each sector might wish to work on first, second, third, and so forth in improving employee perceptions.

Having established that organizational capacity is linked to organizational effectiveness, the next question is whether organizational effectiveness is linked to broader confidence. As we see shortly, perceived effectiveness is firmly related to public confidence in nonprofits. However, perceived effectiveness is also strongly related to confidence among nonprofit employees. Simply put, the more a nonprofit employee believes his or her organization does a good job running its programs and services, spending money wisely, being fair, and helping people, the greater is the likelihood that he or she also trusts the organization to do the right thing just about always. Although being fair in decisions is the most powerful predictor of employee trust, followed by running programs and services, spending money wisely, and helping people, all four create a powerful explanation for why employees do or do not trust their organization.[11]

At least for nonprofit employees, organizational capacity shapes organizational effectiveness, which in turn shapes confidence. Although the linkages are all built on employee perceptions, they are strong linkages nonetheless and not easily discounted.

The Link between Organizational Effectiveness and Public Confidence

Public confidence is essential to the nation's 1.5 million nonprofits and the 12 million Americans they employ. Confidence clearly affects the public's willingness to donate time and money, shapes the political and regulatory environment that governs nonprofits, and has at least some influence on morale within the nonprofit work force. According to the survey of nonprofit employees discussed in the next section of this chapter, 85 percent of employees who said that the word "trusted" described their organization very well also said that morale among their coworkers was either very or somewhat high, compared with just 25 percent of employees who said the word did not describe their organization well.

Confidence, or the lack thereof, also whets the public's appetite for scandal. In the past year alone, the public has been treated to stories about lavish spending at some of the nation's leading philanthropies, improper payments at the United Way of the National Capital Area, conflicts of interest at the Nature Conservancy, the firing of new YWCA president and feminist leader Patricia Ireland after just six months on the job, and countless stories about local charities gone wrong. In turn, these investigations have sparked legislative investigations and calls for tighter regulation, most recently from the California state attorney general, who joined his colleagues in Minnesota and New York in calling for a new era in nonprofit accountability and the legislation to create it. Where the media go, Congress, state attorneys general, and watchdog groups are sure to follow.

Tracking the Decline

Prior to September 11, 2001, public confidence in nonprofits was generally high and largely unqualified.[12] Americans gave the benefit of the doubt to the nonprofit sector despite occasional high-profile scandals such as the United Way and New Era scandals of the 1990s and never wavered in believing that nonprofits play a major role in making communities better places to live.[13]

Unfortunately, public confidence in nonprofits was shaken in the weeks and months following the terrorist attacks on New York City and Washington and has yet to rebound two years later. Americans were watching closely as the Red Cross and other charities came under fire for moving too slowly to disburse billions in September 11 relief funds and did not like what they saw. Asked how closely they were following the controversy surrounding the relief funds in early December 2001, 60 percent of Americans answered "very closely" or "fairly closely," putting the story 25–30 percentage points behind the ongoing coverage of the terrorist attacks and the war in Afghanistan but almost 40 percentage points ahead of an emerging accounting scandal at a Houston energy company called Enron (34 percent).

According to four post–September 11 surveys conducted by Princeton Survey Research Associates on behalf of the Center for Public Service, the percentage of Americans who said they had "a lot" of confidence in nonprofits fell from 25 percent in July 2001 to 18 percent in May 2002, while the percentage who said they had "none" rose from 8 to 17 percent.[14] These changes not only are statistically significant, but they also

TABLE 2-2. Level of Confidence in Nonprofits, 2001–02[a]
Percent of respondents

| Level of | 2001 | | 2002 | | |
confidence	July	December	May	August	September
A lot	25	24	18	19	18
Some	65	62	63	62	64
None	8	11	17	16	15
Sample size	4,216	519	1,737	487	1,063

Source: Surveys conducted by Princeton Survey Research Associates on behalf of the Center for Public Service.
a. Does not include respondents who refused to answer the question or answered "don't know."

are confirmed in two additional surveys conducted in August and September 2002 (see table 2-2 for the trend line from July 2001 to September 2002).

The decline is all the more significant because it came during a period in which confidence in virtually every other civic institution was up. The percentage of Americans who trusted the government in Washington to do the right thing just about always or most of the time increased from 29 percent in July 2001 to 57 percent in October, while the percentages who felt very or somewhat favorable toward government officials all jumped significantly. Favorability toward President Bush increased the most, rising 24 percentage points between July and October, followed by presidential appointees (up 19 points), Vice President Cheney (up 17 points), members of Congress (13 points), and federal government workers (7 points). Even business corporations and the news media showed gains, rising 4 and 10 points, respectively.[15]

Individual Americans also felt better about civic life in general. As Robert Putnam reported in a February 2002 article titled "Bowling Together," "Americans don't only trust political institutions more: We also trust one another more, from neighbors to coworkers to shop clerks, and perfect strangers. . . . In fact, in the wake of terrorist attacks, more Americans reported having cooperated with their neighbors to resolve common problems. Fewer of us feel completely isolated socially, in the sense of having no one to turn to in a personal crisis."[16]

By May 2002, all of these institutions had given back half or more of their post–September 11 gain. Trust in government fell 17 percentage points from its October high, while favorability toward Bush fell 8 points, presidential appointees fell 10 points, Cheney fell 5 points, members of Congress fell 9 points, and federal government workers fell 7 points.

Although the news media held onto half of its small surge, business corporations gave up their 4 percentage point gain and posted an additional 5 point loss, no doubt because of the long list of accounting scandals.

In contrast, confidence in nonprofits showed no gain between July and December and plenty of decline by May. Americans might have felt better about civic life, but they did not feel better about nonprofits. As Putnam also reported, the spike in civic awareness and trust did not lead individuals "to run out and join community organizations or to show up for club meetings they used to shun. Generally speaking, attitudes (such as trust and concern) have shifted more than behavior has."

It is quite possible that confidence in nonprofits surged upward immediately after September 11 as Americans rallied to help. According to an August 2002 survey of 1,000 Americans conducted on behalf of the *Chronicle of Philanthropy*, two-thirds of the public contributed money to the September 11 relief effort, most of it coming in small donations.[17] It would be no surprise to discover that the giving both reflected and affected confidence in nonprofits.

But what might have gone up with the giving was back down by December, no doubt because of the intense coverage of the disbursement controversies. The giving created an intense connection to the relief effort, which helps to explain the 60 percent of Americans who said they were paying very or fairly close attention to the disbursement controversy, which in turn helps to explain the decline in confidence, which in turn contributed to the decline in confidence in nonprofits. Asked in the August 2002 *Chronicle of Philanthropy* survey to look back on the controversy, 42 percent of Americans said the handling of donations had given them less confidence in charities, compared with 19 percent who said it had created more confidence. Although the survey was conducted almost a year after September 11, the self-reporting tracks quite closely the trends in confidence.

Moreover, even if confidence spiked immediately after September 11, it had fallen back to pre–September 11 levels by December and kept falling through May. What may have gone up with a surge in giving and sympathy quickly came down and has yet to rebound more than two years later.

Questions of Wording

Writing in mid-summer 2002, researchers at Independent Sector, a nonprofit coalition of donors and agencies, looked at much of the same data presented above and concluded that there was no cause for alarm.

Whereas I had written that the disbursement controversy had "acted as a brake on public confidence, freezing it at its pre-September levels," Independent Sector took the same data and concluded that confidence was already so high that there "may not have been much room for improvement."[18]

Independent Sector was so sure of its conclusion that it titled its report *Keeping the Trust*. Drawing on a July 2002 survey showing that 64 percent of Americans believed that most charities were honest and ethical in their use of donated funds, its researchers concluded, "Support for nonprofits has remained fairly stable over the last decade, with the events of September 11 having had no lasting impact on the public view of American charities and current scandals in the corporate sector having no apparent negative impact thus far." Even if there was potential erosion, Independent Sector concluded that new sanctions at the Internal Revenue Service and recent efforts to curb abuses were "helping to restore levels of public trust in nonprofit organizations, despite growing public concern over the accountability of for-profit corporations and media reports of problems at a few nonprofit groups."[19]

My worries and Independent Sector's calm were based almost entirely on different combinations of the "a lot," "some," and "none at all" answers. Whereas I focused on separate movement in the "a lot" or "none at all" categories of confidence, Independent Sector combined the "a lot" or "some" categories into an overwhelmingly reassuring measure of confidence. Independent Sector assumed that "some" confidence was all positive confidence, while I assumed that some confidence was a mix of both positive and negative.

My assumption turned out to be right. When respondents were given four options for answering the confidence question in the September 2002 survey, 13 percent said they had a great deal of confidence in nonprofits, 47 percent said they had a fair amount, 26 percent said they had not too much, and 11 percent said they had none at all. Simply put, roughly a third of "some" confidence turned out to be negative.

The numbers should have set off alarms across the sector. At the time, nonprofits were slightly below the judicial branch and executive branch in total confidence, were behind the legislative branch, and were tied with elected and appointed public officials who run government. To the extent a sector is known by the company it keeps, the nonprofit sector had joined a less admired group.

The discomfort should have been amplified by the lack of confidence among two key groups: those who were the most likely to need the sector's help, meaning those with less education and lower incomes, and those who were the most able to give the sector time and money, meaning older Americans with four years of college or more:

—55 percent of respondents with a high school education or less said they had a great deal or a fair amount of confidence in nonprofits, compared with 68 percent of their college-educated peers.

—53 percent of respondents in households with $20,000 or less in annual income expressed a great deal or a fair amount of confidence, compared with 68 percent of respondents in households with income over $60,000.

—48 percent of Americans older than sixty years of age said they had a great deal or a fair amount of confidence in nonprofits, compared with 65 percent of Americans younger than thirty.

These patterns become even more troublesome when age, education, and income are combined. Within each age group, college-educated, high-income Americans are always more confident in their attitude toward nonprofits than their less-educated, lower-income peers. However, across age groups, older, college-educated, high-income Americans are always less confident than their younger peers. Even as education and income increase confidence, aging weakens it. In the long term, therefore, recent increases in access to college should increase confidence in nonprofits. In the short term, however, aging is likely to work its will on the huge baby boom generation. From a purely demographic standpoint, holding all other things equal, confidence in nonprofits is likely to trend downward over the next ten to twenty years.

It is much too early to tell whether demography will be destiny for the nonprofit sector. What is clear is that the impact of September 11 was still visible in public opinion in August and October 2003 and in January 2004. Although confidence edged up slightly in the October 2003 survey, the change was well within the plus-or-minus 3 percent margin of error that comes from using random samples of Americans to represent the population as a whole. Moreover, the January figures suggest that confidence in nonprofits was relatively stable during the period (see table 2-3 for the figures).

Reference Points

The American public relates to the nonprofit sector in many ways, whether as clients, donors, board members, volunteers, or newspaper

TABLE 2-3. Level of Confidence in Nonprofits, 2002–04[a]
Percent of respondents

Answer	September 2002	2003		January 2004
		August	October	
A great deal	13	12	18	13
A fair amount	47	48	45	49
Not too much	26	27	27	25
None	11	10	7	9
Sample size	1,381	1,075	770	6,000

Source: Surveys conducted by Princeton Survey Research Associates on behalf of the Center for Public Service.
a. Does not include respondents who refused to answer the question or answered "don't know."

readers. When asked at the very start of the October survey what the term charitable organization meant to them, 11 percent could not or would not answer the question, 39 percent gave the name of a specific organization, and 50 percent provided an initial description of some kind.

Of the respondents who answered the question with the name of an organization, 20 percent mentioned a church, synagogue, or mosque, 17 percent mentioned the Red Cross, 14 percent mentioned the United Way, 10 percent mentioned the Salvation Army, 6 percent mentioned cancer societies, 4 percent mentioned children's groups, 3 percent mentioned the March of Dimes, 3 percent mentioned heart associations, 2 percent mentioned police and firefighter groups, with the rest spread over a long list of organizations.

Of the respondents who answered the question with a more detailed description of some kind, just over half talked about money in some way:

—36 percent mentioned money either in a positive or at least not in an explicitly negative way, using phrases such as "raising money for a cause," "giving money," giving "gifts, donations," "someone wanting money," "giving money to a good cause," and "collecting money to help other people."

—15 percent mentioned money in a negative way, providing definitions such as "people at the top taking all the money," "fraud," "spending money that is not theirs," "rip-off," "begging money," and "scam."

—21 percent mentioned helping people in some way, answering "somebody who does good work," "someone who is trying to help someone else," someone who is "helping people," someone who is doing "good deeds," and "an organization that exists to help people."

—15 percent used some variation of the terms "nonprofit" or "charity."

—19 percent did not provide an answer that fits into any category, suggesting that they simply did not know what the term charitable organization meant.

When these respondents were asked what organizations they were thinking about when they gave their descriptions, two-thirds provided a name, while one-third could not or would not answer the follow-up question.

When all the answers are totaled, a third of Americans defined the term "charitable organization" through the name of a specific nonprofit organization, another quarter described it in terms of money, a sixth described it using another term such as "nonprofit" or "helping people," a sixth could not answer the question at all, and a tenth described it as a religious institution.

The results generally confirm Salamon's view that "the public remains largely in the dark about how nonprofit organizations actually operate in contemporary America." They also support his view that the sector should abandon the "ritualistic celebration of charitable giving and volunteerism" in favor of a more realistic portrait of nonprofit life that helps Americans to understand the constant pressure to raise money.[20]

Thus respondents who could name an organization at any point in the question were more favorable toward the sector as a whole than respondents who could describe the sector but could not or would not name an organization. Thus respondents who named an organization were twice as likely as those who could not name an organization in the follow-up to express a great deal of confidence in nonprofits (22 versus 11 percent) and were more likely to say that nonprofits did a very good job at running their programs and services (23 versus 17 percent), helping people (37 versus 31 percent), and being fair in their decisions (17 versus 7 percent).

The results also suggest that nonprofits can change public opinion. Having spent the first half of 2002 dealing with national controversies, the Red Cross and the United Way both launched broad improvement efforts designed to reassure and educate donors. The trend lines suggest that the efforts paid off. The percentage of Americans who expressed a great deal or a fair amount of confidence in the Red Cross rose from 78 percent in September 2002 to 82 percent in October 2003, while the percentage who expressed not too much or no confidence at all in the United Way fell from 35 to 31 percent over the same period.

The United Way may be the more interesting case, especially given its recent efforts to transform the language it uses to explain itself to the public. In 2003 the United Way of America urged its 1,400 independent local affiliates to become "community impact United Ways." After acknowledging that every indicator showed declining market share in its communities, Brian Gallagher, United Way of America's president and chief executive officer, urged his colleagues to abandon the traditional language of federated appeal:

> We are moving from only funding the needs of agencies and programs to investing in strategies for community change and in new partnerships to define and implement those strategies. We are moving from a focus on program outcomes to a focus also on community outcomes, named and framed by the community itself. We are moving from "dollars raised" to "community results" as our measure of success. We are moving from an organization through which people give money to one that people also experience as the best way to get involved in their communities.[21]

Becoming a community impact United Way involves more than just language and better measures, however. It also means more donor involvement in the decision to give, meaning more opportunities to direct funds to one or more of four specific impact goals: helping children and youth succeed, strengthening families, promoting self-sufficiency, and promoting safe and healthy communities. At the Atlanta United Way, potential donors are told to "choose your impact"; at the United Way of the Massachusetts Bay Area, donors choose among "targeted funds" for "keeping kids on track," "success by 6," "today's girls . . . tomorrow's leaders," "care for our elderly," "feed and shelter our hungry and homeless," "prevent cancer," "prevent HIV/AIDS," and "protect women and children from abuse" before getting the long list of "restricted contributions" to specific organizations. Recent experience suggests that donors prefer the broad "targeted" choice over the restricted choice.

The community impact option clearly fits with the growing concerns discussed below. But United Ways could go even further in reassuring donors and volunteers that they are picking high-performing organizations in each of the targeted areas. If donors and volunteers have become social investors of a kind, United Ways and other intermediary organizations must be willing to put at least some of their money to work in both achieving and sustaining high performance. Just as investors will stay with a mutual fund that consistently picks winners, donors and volunteers will stay with United Ways that provide both choices and reassurance that they are investing in high performance.

Americans do not have to pass a literacy test to form opinions about the nonprofit sector, however, or to give money and volunteer. Moreover, other questions in the survey suggest that Americans have a generally accurate sense of where the nonprofit sector begins and ends. Whereas 90 percent of respondents said the Red Cross was a charitable organization, 67 percent said the National Rifle Association was not. No matter how they reach their opinions, Americans are no longer willing to give the sector the benefit of the doubt, especially when it comes to spending money wisely.

Sources of Doubt

Unlike recent surveys of confidence, which have been limited to a handful of questions tacked onto other surveys, the October 2003 survey was long enough to allow a deeper examination of public opinion. The survey showed more than just stagnation in confidence. It also revealed significant public doubts about how nonprofits deliver services, help people, work, and spend money:

—14 percent of respondents said nonprofits did a very good job at spending money wisely, compared with 28 percent who said they did not do too good a job or did a job that was not at all good and 46 percent who said that they did a somewhat good job.

—18 percent said nonprofits did a very good job at being fair in their decisions, compared with 17 percent who said they did not do too good a job or did not do a good job at all and 52 percent who said they did a somewhat good job.

—21 percent said nonprofits did a very good job at running their programs and services, compared with 18 percent who said they did not do too good a job or did not do a good job at all and 53 percent who said they did a somewhat good job.

—34 percent said nonprofits did a very good job at helping people, compared with 12 percent who said they did not do too good a job or did not do a good job at all and 50 percent who said they did a somewhat good job.

These figures produce an enormous credibility gap between what the public and employees believe about nonprofit organizations. As table 2-4

TABLE 2-4. Perception of Nonprofits as Doing a Very Good Job, by Task[a]
Percent of respondents specified

Task	Americans	Nonprofit employees	Gap
Running programs and services	21	56	+35
Spending money wisely	14	44	+30
Being fair in decisions	18	45	+28
Helping people	34	73	+39
Sample size	770	1,140	

Source: October 2003 telephone survey of Americans and 2001 survey of employees.

shows, either nonprofit employees are desperately wrong or the public is woefully mistaken.

The survey also revealed two other harbingers of declining confidence: waste and executive pay. Among respondents, 46 percent said the leaders of nonprofits were paid too much, 27 percent said they were paid about the right amount, and just 8 percent said they were paid too little. In addition, 20 percent of respondents said nonprofits wasted a great deal of money, another 40 percent said they wasted a fair amount, 30 percent said they did not waste too much, and just 3 percent said nonprofits wasted no money.

These perceptions of waste tainted even the modest positives in the ratings of effectiveness. Thus 41 percent of respondents who said nonprofits did a very good job at helping people, 39 percent who said nonprofits did a very good job at running their programs and services, and 32 percent who said nonprofits did a very good job at being fair in their decisions also said nonprofits wasted a great deal or a fair amount of money. The tainting held even for respondents who said nonprofits did a very good job at spending money wisely, 34 percent of whom also said nonprofits wasted a great deal or a fair amount of money.

Further analysis suggests that confidence is tightly linked to public views of nonprofit effectiveness in their programs and services, spending money wisely, being fair in their decisions, and helping people. For example, 68 percent of respondents who said nonprofits did a very good job at helping people also expressed a great deal of confidence in nonprofits, while 78 percent of respondents who said nonprofits did not do a good job at all in helping people also said they had no confidence in nonprofits. The relationships were similarly tight in the other three measures of nonprofit performance. Simply put, the less respondents thought of nonprofit performance, the less confidence they expressed.

Confidence in the Red Cross and United Way also affected overall confidence in nonprofits. The more confidence respondents had in these two brand names, the more confidence they had in nonprofits overall.

Confidence also varied with views of nonprofit waste and executive pay. Respondents who said nonprofits wasted little or no money had much more confidence than those who said nonprofits wasted a great deal or a fair amount of money, while those who said nonprofit executives were paid about the right amount or too little had much more confidence than those who said nonprofit executives were paid too much.

Finally, confidence varied with what I call discretionary giving and volunteering, which means giving and volunteering to organizations *other* than one's church, mosque, synagogue, and alma mater. Although it is not clear whether confidence leads to discretionary giving and volunteering, or vice versa, the link is unmistakable. Thus 77 percent of respondents who said they had a great deal of confidence in nonprofits donated money to a nonprofit other than their church, synagogue, mosque, or college, compared with 51 percent who said they had no confidence at all. Similarly, 44 percent of respondents who expressed a great deal of confidence volunteered with a nonprofit other than their church, synagogue, mosque, or college, compared with 21 percent who said they had no confidence at all in nonprofits.

The link between confidence and discretionary giving and volunteering is confirmed in further statistical analysis designed to pit competing explanations against each other. Household income emerges as the number one statistically significant predictor of discretionary giving (higher income increases the likelihood of discretionary giving), followed by education (higher education increases the likelihood), confidence in nonprofits (higher confidence increases the likelihood), age (being older increases the likelihood), and race (being white increases the likelihood), while education is the number one predictor of discretionary volunteering (higher education increases the likelihood), followed by confidence in nonprofits (higher confidence increases the likelihood of volunteering).[22]

The Link between Perceived Effectiveness and Confidence

If confidence matters to time and money, the question becomes, What matters to confidence? It is possible, for example, that confidence in nonprofits is a product of social trust. Perhaps individuals who think most people try to be helpful also believe that nonprofits do the same; perhaps individuals who do not trust strangers do not trust strange nonprofits.

It is also quite possible that confidence in nonprofits is related to party identification. After all, the Bush administration has campaigned hard to open federal grants to faith-based institutions, arguing that secular organizations are not as compassionate as religious institutions. Perhaps Republicans share the president's disquiet.

Finally, it is most certainly possible that public anger about waste and executive pay is so intense that these two inflammatory issues crowd out all other considerations. Perhaps individuals simply cannot see past the scandals.

Once again, further statistical analysis provides a way to sort competing explanations. As above, one cannot test every possible explanation simultaneously without jeopardizing the validity of the results. However, as box 2-2 shows, organizational effectiveness is the most powerful predictor among eighteen possible explanations for confidence: the respondent's rating of how good a job nonprofits do in (1) running their programs and services, (2) spending money wisely, (3) being fair in decisions, and (4) helping people; the respondent's sense that (5) most people can be trusted, (6) most people try to take advantage of him or her, and (7) people try to be helpful most of the time; (8) the respondent's memory of being warned not to trust certain kinds of people; (9) the respondent's rating of how much money nonprofits waste; (10) the respondent's sense that nonprofit leaders are paid too much; the respondent's (11) sex, (12) race, (13) education, (14) age, (15) household income, and (16) political party identification; and the respondent's confidence in (17) the Red Cross and (18) the United Way.

As box 2-2 shows, eight of the eighteen explanations have a significant bearing on confidence. Spending money wisely emerges as the top predictor of confidence, followed by helping people and running programs and services. Confidence in the Red Cross emerges as a poor fourth, while neither being fair in decisions nor having confidence in the United Way is significant.

This analysis suggests a clear strategy for improving public confidence, and it is most definitely *not* to change programs, unleash more watchdogs, let the big brand names do the heavy lifting for the rest of the sector, or cap executive salaries. Indeed, further analysis suggests that public opinion about nonprofit waste and executive pay are more a consequence than a cause of confidence. Thus respondents who had no

---

BOX 2-2. Statistically Significant Explanations of Public Confidence in Nonprofits

Based on a sample size of 770, the following explanations of public confidence in nonprofits are statistically significant:

1. Believing that nonprofits do a good job at spending money wisely,

2. Believing that nonprofits do a good job at helping people,

3. Believing that nonprofits do a good job at running programs and services,

4. Having confidence in the Red Cross,

5. Education (greater education = higher confidence),

6. Race (being white = higher confidence),

7. Age (being young = higher confidence),

8. Sex (being female = higher confidence).

Note: These results were produced through ordinary least-squares regression of confidence in nonprofits in the October 2003 survey. Strength is measured using standardized beta weights, and significance is based on t tests, which indicate the chance that a given result is not the result of random occurrence. The adjusted R^2 for the overall model is 0.410, meaning that the analysis explains roughly 41 percent of the variation in public confidence toward nonprofits, a strong result that is significant at the 0.000 level.

---

confidence in nonprofits were twice as likely as those who had a great deal of confidence to say that nonprofit leaders were overpaid and five times more likely to say that nonprofits wasted a great deal of money.

Rather, the analysis underscores the importance of organizational effectiveness. Since nonprofits can do little to change the overall education, race, age, and sex of the population, they can either put their hopes in the Red Cross, which may or may not actually improve confidence in their own organization, or take action to improve public perceptions that they are spending money wisely, helping people, and running their programs and services effectively. The latter course may be more difficult, but it will almost surely prove more effective in the long run, especially given the extraordinary impact of spending money wisely on public confidence. Nevertheless, if Americans believe that the greater problem with nonprofits is inefficiency, not misplaced priorities, it seems reasonable to suggest that one solution would be to reduce inefficiency through capacity-building interventions such as strategic planning, board development, alliances and mergers, employee training, and so forth.

Changing public perceptions about effectiveness is no doubt difficult, especially given unrelenting scrutiny from regulators, Congress, watchdog groups, and the media. Some nonprofits will rightly argue that they are already effective. Others will rightly complain that they simply do not have the time or money to advertise their effectiveness. Still others will rightly suggest that confidence in nonprofits is a collective good that must be generated by organizations and donors working together to reverse perceptions.

But, whether correctly or incorrectly, rightly or wrongly, the public has come to believe that substantial numbers of nonprofits are either not doing well enough or not doing enough good to restore confidence to its pre–September 11 levels. Absent any argument to the contrary, particularly an argument rooted in measures of effectiveness, the credibility gap will remain, while confidence will stay down, as will the volunteering and giving that are clearly linked to it.

Conclusions

For those who believe that public confidence will rebound with the passage of time, the latest data provide little solace. Confidence in charitable organizations remained virtually unchanged from September 2002 to January 2004, while public opinion appeared to harden over time to a much more negative edge.

The good news in the statistics is that the nonprofit sector controls its own destiny. Unlike confidence in government, which is often contaminated by partisanship, confidence in nonprofits is driven by effectiveness. To the extent nonprofits can demonstrate improvement, there is every reason to believe that the public will respond.

This chapter has made a strong case that organizational capacity may be an important lever for changing public perceptions. Organizational capacity clearly makes a difference in how nonprofit employees feel about their work, which, in turn, matters to employee perceptions of their own organization's effectiveness. Assuming that employee perceptions of their organization's effectiveness bear some relationship to public perceptions of nonprofit effectiveness, the link between capacity and confidence is made. The link is not perfect, however, and includes several leaps of faith, most notably the one between how employees and the public perceive effectiveness.

Again, even if organizational capacity has no ultimate impact on public confidence, it is clearly linked to employee perceptions of how well their organization spends money, runs programs, makes decisions, and helps people. To the extent that these perceptions are fair reflections of reality, the link provides more than enough justification for encouraging nonprofits to invest in organizational capacity. Organization does not just matter to how well nonprofits work; it matters greatly. The question for the next chapter is whether such investments have any perceptible rate of return and, if so, why.

3 | The State of Nonprofit Capacity Building

Just because organizational capacity matters to effectiveness does not mean that efforts to strengthen capacity actually work. Indeed, there is very little hard evidence that capacity building produces a significant rate of return on investment, not because capacity building has a dismal record, but because it has almost no measurable record at all. Although there are plenty of stories about how capacity building can change organizational life, including some told in this chapter, there is relatively little evidence of measurable impact.

To the contrary, the available evidence suggests that capacity building in the private sector has a very high rate of failure. Organizational reengineering is believed to collapse roughly half the time, total quality management is often abandoned well before its seven-year tipping point, the vast majority of mergers and acquisitions produce net declines in productivity, three out of four new computer systems do not improve efficiency, new software works only a third of the time, and downsizing almost never generates much downsizing.[1]

The list of disappointments has been growing for decades: a 1993 study of 1,000 downsizing campaigns showed a 19 percent success rate; a second study of 135 "massive restructurings" showed that 50 percent failed to achieve significant increases in value compared with the competition; a 1998 study of 7,500 software upgrades showed a 26 percent "fully successful rate," meaning on time, on budget, and fully functional; a 1998 analysis of restructuring at 5,000 firms between 1986 and 1998 showed that changes in organizational structure through reengineering, flattening, and downsizing had mixed impacts on market share and financial performance; a 2001 study of process reengineering showed a 23 percent success rate; and a 2003 study of major change programs at forty firms showed that 58 percent of the efforts failed to meet their targets.[2]

Even when capacity building succeeds, researchers are not always certain why it worked. As Darrell Rigby, a Bain & Company senior researcher, writes of the recent surge in the use of business management tools, "The term 'management tool' now encompasses a broad spectrum of approaches to management—from simple planning software to complex organizational designs to revised business philosophies. Many of these tools offer conflicting advice. One may call for keeping all your customers, while another advises you to focus only on the most profitable. But all of these tools have one thing in common: they promise to make their users more successful. Today, beleaguered managers—struggling to demonstrate that they can adapt to rapid change in an increasingly challenging world—are turning to management tools in unprecedented numbers."[3]   *The Bottom Line on Management*

Nevertheless, as this chapter shows, the nonprofit sector is doing almost as much capacity building as the private sector. According to the random-sample Internet-based survey of 318 nonprofits on which this chapter is based, nonprofits used an average of ten tools to strengthen organizational capacity during the past few years, which is surprisingly near the pace set by the private firms surveyed by Bain. This chapter draws on the survey to ask what these nonprofits were doing, why they decided to act, and how they did the work.

The Search for Capacity Building

As a term of art, "capacity building" cries out for rigorous measurement. After all, capacity can be contained in organizations and people, imported through education and practice, exported through peer-to-peer learning and rigorous research, and replenished through even more education and practice. If capacity building is the answer, increasing organizational impact is the question.

Effectiveness?

This hope has clearly fueled funding for more capacity building. As Barbara Blumenthal reports, philanthropic funding for technical assistance tripled from $62 million in 1997 to $218 million in 2001, while management development grants quadrupled from $60 million to $218 million.[4] During the same period, membership in Grantmakers for Effective Organizations, an affinity group within the Council on Foundations, expanded dramatically, as did subscriptions to *Nonprofit Quarterly*, a journal devoted to organizational effectiveness, and enrollments in graduate training programs.

Unfortunately, the activity did not produce a parallel increase in evidence-based research on what actually works for strengthening organizational capacity. To the contrary, research funding dropped sharply, in large part because Atlantic Philanthropies and the David and Lucile Packard Foundation left the field. For good or ill, more than $1 million of that funding supported the research featured in this report, including the survey of nonprofit capacity building described below.

The State of the Evidence

In theory, capacity building is designed to change some aspect of an organization's existing environment, internal structure, leadership, and management systems, which, in turn, should improve employee morale, expertise, productivity, efficiency, and so forth, which should strengthen an organization's capacity to do its work, which should increase organizational performance (see figure 3-1 for the logic chain).

In practice, however, there is very little systematic evidence on whether and how capacity building works. It is impossible to know whether capacity building works, for example, without some standardized measure of organizational effectiveness against which to assess impact. Yet, as Daniel Forbes writes in an article titled "Measuring the Unmeasurable," organizational effectiveness remains both a powerful and a problematic concept for researchers: powerful because it can be an essential tool for evaluating and improving the work of organizations, but problematic because it means different things to different people.[5]

Even simple measures of administrative cost mean different things to different people. As Cassandra Benjamin convincingly shows, the nonprofit sector and its regulators have yet to agree on a common definition of just what constitutes an administrative cost. Under current law, the Internal Revenue Service requires nonprofits with annual gross receipts of at least $25,000 to sort their management, fund-raising, and program

FIGURE 3-1. Linkages between Organizational Capacity and Effectiveness

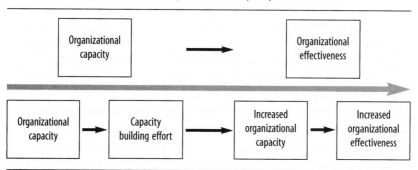

expenses into separate categories. However, the filing instructions provide more than enough leeway to disguise administrative and fund-raising expenses as program expenses, casting serious doubts on the sorting of data. Although recent research suggests that the overall revenue and expenditure data are accurate, the sorting of expenditure data is often designed to show the lowest possible administrative and fund-raising costs.[6]

The incentives for creative interpretation are obvious: Donors and watchdog groups often use administrative costs to compare nonprofits. Thus the American Institute of Philanthropy gives letter grades to a limited sample of nonprofits based on three criteria: (1) total revenues devoted to an organization's charitable purpose, (2) the cost of raising each $100 of funding, and (3) years of available assets. Although the institute acknowledges that there are many factors in the giving decision, it believes that at least 60 percent of revenues should be devoted to programs, no more than 35 percent should be spent on fund-raising, and groups with more than three years of available assets are among the least needy. In fact, the institute gives an automatic "F" to any organization with more than five years of reserves.

The Better Business Bureau's Wise Giving Alliance also uses similar financial data in awarding its National Charity Seal to individual nonprofits. Nonprofits can only receive and use the seal by meeting twenty separate standards, five of which involve qualitative judgments of some kind, including adequate board oversight, financial accuracy, truthful reporting, donor privacy, and responsiveness to complaints. Another thirteen involve minimum yes-no standards, including board size (at least five voting members), number of meetings (at least three a year), compensation (no more than 10 percent of board members may be compensated), material conflicts of interest (none), performance assessment and effectiveness (a written assessment every two years), financial reserves (no more than three times the past year's expenses or three times the current year's budget, whichever is higher), financial reporting (public), annual report (public and Internet accessible), and disclosure of benefits from the sale of products or services (public). The only two standards that involve quantitative data are based on the flawed cost data: (1) the organization should spend at least 65 percent of its total expenses on program activities, and (2) the organization should not spend more than 35 percent of related contributions on fund-raising.

Although there is much to admire in the list, most notably the new focus on performance and effectiveness, the seal does not impose a set of uniform reporting definitions for the three most visible components: program expenses, fund-raising expenses, and reserves. Thus nonprofits can play the same games with the Wise Giving Alliance that they sometimes do with the Internal Revenue Service and donors. As Jennifer Lammers writes of the financial ratios used in the Wise Giving Alliance ratings, "The resulting pressure on nonprofit managers leads to increasingly creative allocations of expenses, further muddying the true performance picture. Even worse, some nonprofits adhere to bare-bones administrative budgets that actually jeopardize the organization's stability and hinder its ability to grow or respond to change."[7]

This creativity also raises reasonable suspicions about hidden waste—suspicions that eventually wind their way into public opinion about the sector's ability to spend money wisely. As Benjamin writes, "Beyond the question of whether a lower rate is always better, there is a more fundamental problem with published administrative cost rates. Within the nonprofit sector, there is great variation in the definitions of terms related to administrative costs, as well as in the methods used to calculate the administrative cost percentages. . . . As a result, the published administrative cost rates cannot easily be compared between organizations and mean little on their own when the calculation methods used are unknown."[8]

Coupled with pressure to spend as little as possible on administration, the lack of standards leads some organizations either to lie about their cost structure or to starve themselves. The practice is easy to understand, writes Clara Miller, president and CEO of the Nonprofit Finance Fund, which has made more than $70 million in loans to help nonprofits strengthen their capital base and improve financial management over the past twenty years:

> Givers, almost invariably well-meaning, generous individuals or foundations, often imagine that this practice improves the likelihood that more money will be spent on services and increases the number served. Actually, this practice only accomplishes two things: it increases the likelihood that the dedicated manager will lie to protect the people served, or it encourages the manager to seriously underinvest in support and systems, thereby undermining the entire operation and eventually the quality of services. The irony is that these money rules end up undermining program quality most consistently among the best and the brightest: the innovative small programs with important successes, which are going to scale.[9]

How else is one to explain the Urban Institute's recent finding that 37 percent of nonprofit organizations with private contributions of at least $50,000 reported that they spent exactly nothing on fund-raising on their Internal Revenue Service Form 990 revenue and expense statements? Consider how the Urban Institute answers these questions:

> While ignorance, sloppiness, or lack of capacity might explain or excuse poor reporting by public charities, there is another more insidious force at work as well. That is, while charities are not given many incentives to accurately track and report their financials, they *are* faced with incentives to report inaccurately. Since Form 990 is the only public document required of charities, the Form has become increasingly available and its figures increasingly used to compare the donation-worthiness of charities. As a result, these same charities are faced with the prospect of managing what they report so as to look positive on the various measures of financial efficiency. Some give in to the pressure to fudge the numbers.[10]

Perceptions of Performance

Absent more reliable expenditure sorting, scholars must rely on perceptions of impact to assess performance. Acknowledging the bias in such perceptions, at least one can claim that agreement is emerging on what constitutes organizational effectiveness. When asked what the words meant to them in 2001, for example, half of my *Pathways to Nonprofit Effectiveness* executives used the word "mission" somewhere in their definition, and two-thirds focused on measurable outcomes. Respondents gave a variety of answers. One simply answered, "all the components in place that will enable you to go forward with your mission," another said, "being able to have the desired impact," and still others said, "doing what we preach," "producing demonstrable results," "using resources to get the greatest impact," and "showing that you achieve a little more than you set out to do." One respondent put it all together as follows: "In essence, we are providing effective services that are outcomes driven; we manage our money well, hold public trust high, and put the focus on issues of performance and developing appropriate services."

Moreover, nonprofits have clearly become much better at describing the outcomes or results they seek, in no small part because of the unrelenting encouragement from the United Way of America. McKinsey and Company has also made progress toward designing a grid for measuring organizational capacity, while the Roberts Enterprise Development Fund has advanced the concept of "investment philanthropy," which is built around basic definitions of value and social return on investment.[11] The sector may not be that far away from relatively precise measures of both capacity and performance.

For the time being, however, the sector is still highly dependent on assertions in making the case for capacity building. The assertions may be grounded in decades of organizational research, but they often involve leaps of faith between the private and nonprofit sectors and eagerness to resolve tensions that still exist in the research literature.[12] Some studies do, indeed, show that investments in information technology can produce 50 to 60 percent rates of return on investment, but other studies show no linkage at all or negative rates of return.[13] Some studies do suggest that standards of excellence can strengthen everything from customer satisfaction to productivity, but others suggest null or negative effects from adopting the certification programs that often accompany a standards program.[14]

The Capacity-Building Survey

The following analysis of organizational capacity building is based on an Internet survey of 318 nonprofits completed in 2003. As a group, the 318 organizations covered a wide range of nonprofit missions, including education, children and youth services, health, general human services, housing and homelessness, arts and culture, job training or economic and community development, environment, and science. Most were local organizations, a majority were more than sixteen years old, three-quarters employed less than 100 people, and roughly two-fifths had budgets under $1 million. The survey questionnaire and overall answers are presented in appendix A to this book.

The survey started with a random sample of 3,000 organizations with annual revenues of at least $250,000.[15] The sample was generated by GuideStar, which maintains a list of more than 850,000 nonprofits that file annual tax returns with the Internal Revenue Service. The executive director or president of each nonprofit was contacted by first-class letter, given a unique password to the survey website, and encouraged to participate on three additional occasions, first by postcard, then by first-class letters. The survey website was accessible from March 27 to August 12, 2003.

Of the 3,000 addresses on the list, 179 were undeliverable, leaving a total sample size of 2,821. Of the 2,821 eligible respondents, 381 (14 percent) went to the website, and 318 (11 percent) finished the questionnaire. This low response rate prompted a telephone survey of 150 nonrespondents to find out why they did not participate, which, in turn, suggested that roughly a quarter of the 3,000 organizations had disappeared by the time of the survey, moved without a forwarding address, were ineligible for the survey, or were in some state of organizational transition at the time of the survey. According to the nonrespondents survey, another quarter lost the invitation or never received it in the first place.[16] Once the half of the original sample that apparently did not receive the invitations was excluded, the adjusted response rate for the capacity-building survey rose to a healthier 22 percent.

The critical question is not whether the response rate was very low or somewhat low, however, but whether the final sample of 318 respondents who filled out the full capacity-building survey represented the larger population of eligible nonprofits from which they were drawn. Simply asked, what can the 318 organizations represented in the survey say to the rest of the sector? The survey of nonrespondents suggests two answers.

First, a substantial number of nonprofits are engaged in some kind of capacity building. Although it is impossible to give an exact number, roughly two-thirds of nonprofits may be doing something to improve their organization's performance at any given time.[17] Asked whether they were doing anything in particular to improve their organization's performance, just five of the eighty-one respondents said they were not doing much in the way of capacity building: two said they were in survival mode, two said they were doing things pretty much the same way as always, and one could not give any examples of capacity building. Of the seventy-six who said they were working to improve their organization's performance, 87 percent provided two examples, and 53 percent provided three. Investments in new technology were the most common form of capacity building (twenty-two mentions), followed by strategic planning (twenty), staff training (seventeen), fund-raising and board development (fourteen mentions each), and reorganization (twelve).

Second, a substantial proportion of nonprofits that engaged in capacity building gave high marks to the effort. Asked about the success of their organization's most recent effort, seventeen respondents rated the effort as completely or mostly successful in improving their organization's performance, forty-five respondents said the effort was somewhat successful or less, and fourteen respondents said the effort was still under way.

Caveats about Measurement

These surveys do not add up to a "census" of capacity building across the sector or answer questions about the lack of capacity building. Moreover, the vast majority of nonprofits are much smaller than the organizations covered by the survey: less than 10 percent of all tax-exempt organizations have budgets at or over $250,000, which means that activity levels among smaller nonprofits may be lower.

However, the general conclusion of the survey is applicable to nonprofits of all sizes and missions: capacity building can be a high-yield, low-cost investment that enhances program performance. The question for the following pages is what can be done to improve the odds that capacity building will actually contribute to capacity. Capacity building is often funded internally, whether through operating support or other discretionary accounts. Much of it is also done with little or no contact with the outside world, whether through a workshop, the Internet, or a conversation with a peer. If nonprofits are going to invest scarce resources in capacity building, they ought to invest wisely.

The organizations represented embraced an extraordinary range of missions. Asked what kind of work their organization did, 32 percent said education services, 31 percent said children and youth services, 21 percent said health, 17 percent said general human services, 17 said housing or homelessness, 15 percent said arts and culture, 11 percent said job training or economic or community development, 9 percent said nutrition or hunger, 7 percent said environment, and 31 percent gave additional specifics—for example, HIV/AIDS, refugee services, domestic abuse prevention, adoption assistance, educational radio, youth camps, and so forth. As if to confirm the diversity, more than half of the respondents checked two of the eleven boxes describing their work, while a third checked three.

Although it is tempting to focus on differences, the 318 organizations also shared certain characteristics. The vast majority of the respondents—81 percent—said they worked for a local nonprofit, while just 17 percent worked for a national nonprofit, and 7 percent worked for an international one. In addition, the organizations shared very similar clientele: 81 percent said the word "diverse" described the people they served very or somewhat well, followed by "low-income" (69 percent) and "disadvantaged," "children and/or families," and "urban" (68 percent each).

It would hardly be surprising to find that capacity building varied with mission and clientele. Although the sample size was much too small to compare interventions across different missions, this project involved an effort to identify enough additional low-income-serving children or family organizations to permit meaningful analysis of whether and how they build capacity. A summary of this analysis is presented in appendix B. For now, suffice it to say that low-income-serving children and family organizations are often very much like other nonprofits in their capacity building except in two areas. They are more likely to report that they have outside funding for their capacity building and also more likely to report they do not have adequate resources for their capacity-building effort. They may be getting outside support, but rarely enough to push their efforts past the tipping point for success.

The rest of this chapter asks just how they can improve the odds that the capacity building will fit their needs and will succeed. It also examines the linkages between capacity building and organizational effectiveness. If the linkages do not exist, nonprofits would be better off spending their time, money, and energy on their core programs. But if the linkages are clear and the effects significant, perhaps nonprofits, their boards, and donors should invest even more.

Defining Capacity Building

At its most basic level, capacity building can be defined as any effort to increase, replenish, or improve an organization's capacity. However, before asking what nonprofits have been doing to strengthen their organizations, it is important to note that many of the 318 respondents surveyed used capacity building to describe different steps in the logic chain described above. Asked early in the Internet survey what the term capacity building meant to them, respondents gave four broad answers:

—36 percent of the respondents defined capacity building as a way to increase organizational resources or inputs. One respondent said that the term meant "obtaining or developing strategies to have the resources necessary to serve your clients." Another talked about "having the ability to raise money, garner support, and increase visibility within the community it serves," and others pointed to "providing people with the tools and skills they need to be more productive, efficient, and effective in their work," "developing resources to meet goals," "undertaking activities designed to solidify an organization's infrastructure to accommodate expansion," "finding resources to provide more effective services: sometimes money that can be directly applied to specific needs, sometimes capabilities to respond to growth and new challenges," and "increasing skills, knowledge, ability, resources, and anything that helps a person or an organization be better able to do what either wants to do."

—30 percent defined capacity building as a way to measure an organization's activities. One respondent answered with phrases such as "getting the most bang for your buck" and "being able to serve more people with programs and activities." Another defined the term as "a physical plant, as in greater capacity, or assisting staff to be more prepared, efficient, and productive in their tasks," and others focused on "increasing the number of people that our museum can serve, while also increasing the number of services," "(1) increasing capacity to offer services to more constituents . . . and (2) increasing capacity to offer programs through improved quality and productivity—that is, programmatic capacity versus physical capacity," and "the number of people we can safely handle in our building." Several respondents highlighted basic programmatic reach. As one said, "Capacity means the numbers served, but capacity building means the most efficient and effective means of increasing the number of clients served with limited resources."

—16 percent defined capacity building as a way to improve overall program performance, improve the lives of clients, and increase organizational outputs and outcomes. One respondent answered that it meant "substantially building the depth and breadth of the program to the people served," and another defined the term as "developing programs and services to meet the needs of our visitors." Others used phrases such as "increasing the ability of the organization to meet its mission," "enabling people to help themselves," "helping those less fortunate to lead a normal life," "giving people the skills, information, and networks to make the most of their talents," "creating a more diverse economic base for rural communities and creating programs to get children more active at a young age," and "helping people to increase their chances of success."

—9 percent of the respondents defined capacity building as a way to maximize resources and efficiency. One said that it meant "getting the very best out of what you have" and "maximizing the number of clients we serve at the lowest cost to consumers." Another defined it as "utilizing the resources of your organization to benefit the most people," and others focused on having "the ability to improve services in a depressed economy and with limited staff," using "an organization's physical, financial, and human resources at such a high level of efficiency that the only way to grow is to increase the resources," having the "ability to handle a wide range of situations and problems, to improve a situation for a client," and getting "the most bang for the buck."

Although 10 percent of the sample did not give a definition or rejected the term as just another "bureaucratic buzzword," most of these respondents believed that capacity building was useless unless it improved program results. The link between capacity building and mission was even clearer in longer telephone interviews conducted with eighteen of the 318 respondents in November 2003.

Longer telephone interviews with eighteen respondents conducted by my colleague Elizabeth Hubbard revealed even greater texture in how respondents approached organizational investment.[18] Sometimes, capacity building was described as a necessary evil for success. "I really hate to add non-service capacity," the executive director of a New Hampshire family service program explained. "I tease our administrative staff about all of the useless overhead, so I'm really careful about it. I try to think strategically. Where does this next thing come into capacity? How is it going to pay off for clients? How is the money going to pay off for the organization in a tangible, immediate way? At least in our sector, we don't have the luxury of making investments for the future. It has to be much more tangible and carefully planned to pay off."

The head of a Seattle-based dance company described the trade-off as a pendulum "that swings back and forth between that which is visible, the artistic product, and that which is needed in order to support the creation and operation of the organization that then creates the product. And I think there is a real pendulum swing back and forth as you make investments in dancers and musicians on stage, new products and scenery and costumes, which usually means that you're not paying attention to the other side. After a while, you realize that the quality of what you're putting out there starts to exceed the ability of the infrastructure to support it, and so the pendulum has to swing back the other way."

Other times, capacity building was described as a way to improve funding or as a gateway to understanding a new world. As the head of a Michigan food bank argued, "The hunger issue is just growing, especially in today's economy, and believing in that mission pushes you to try to open up avenues to make sure that we're feeding people. You can't just start new and innovating programs if you're not getting the funding to operate your program. That doesn't make any sense." The director of a Toledo museum agreed: "I know the world has changed, people have changed—what they want to do with it; how they get their information. And museums need to change, too. It's not just the new people, the new audiences. It's also the old people, the old audiences. As people change and grow and learn, their visits to the museum change, too. How does a child get fulfilled and have a life-changing experience when he or she comes to the museum? How does a tourist who is passing through town? How does someone who comes regularly every month?"

Still other times, capacity building was viewed as essential to describing the mission. As the head of a Massachusetts drug treatment program argued, "People ask what happens three, six, nine, or twelve months after discharge. We always used to say, 'We don't know; no one pays us to do that.' Well, guess what? If you're running an efficient organization, you can divert funds from other inefficient processes to this tracking of outcomes, which you can use to go to legislators and talk about the dollars they're spending. And so it's clearly self-serving, but it's what every other smart business does out there." The director of a Minnesota environmental organization also talked about the role of capacity in creating impact: "We were not unhealthy; we were just not living up to our potential. We had a lot of opportunity for growth in our fund-raising, membership, education programs, and our outreach. We were a stagnant organization that had done some really good work, but we really hadn't grown with the times in terms of the conservation movement as a whole. I really looked at us as a little teeny organization that had much greater potential."

Finally, others talked about capacity building as the answer to organizational disaster. Consider how the director of a Georgia-based homeless program described her organization's broad effort to strengthen the board, create a rainy day reserve fund, and start to measure outcomes: "When I got here, the agency was in pretty bad shape and was in debt. So our efforts were all part of moving in a different direction. In the last two years, it became clear that we were stagnant and weren't bringing in the extra cash, the private dollars that we wanted, and obviously the way to do that was to increase the board effectiveness and in order to do that we found a really good consultant who helped and coached on how to do that stuff. It's been a long process, but we're moving in the right direction."

Ultimately, capacity building is best described as part of ordinary good practice. There are times when organizations will need it more and times when they will need it less. But until the world stops changing and the future becomes certain, organizations can either change themselves or be changed by others.

Asked what she had learned from the eighteen executive directors she had interviewed, Hubbard said "They are proud of their efforts to improve their organizations. They want to talk about it. In fact, it can be hard to get them off the phone or to get them to move out of the details of what they did and to talk about the larger issues of the day. By and large, they are not simply content to run their organizations; they are seeking to improve them."

An Inventory of Activity

Whether it is called capacity building, technical assistance, tools of management, organizational change, or plain old common sense, the 318 organizations represented in the survey have been doing a lot of it. When asked to think back over the last five years about what their organization had done to improve its management or programmatic impact, 88 percent said that their organization had done something to improve external relationships, 86 percent said their organization had acted to improve internal structure, 85 percent said their organization had strengthened its internal management systems, and 77 percent said their organization had enhanced its internal leadership.

Within these four categories of organizational improvement, respondents were also asked about twenty-three specific capacity-building activities, ranging from collaboration and mergers to new technology and outcomes measurement. According to the checklist, these nonprofits had been very active, indeed.

—Among the 88 percent who said their organization had worked on external relationships, 85 percent had worked toward greater collaboration, 72 percent had done strategic planning, 65 percent had tried to strengthen fund-raising, 61 percent had engaged in some form of media relations, and 10 percent had participated in a merger.

—Among the 86 percent who said their organization had worked on internal structure, 73 percent had done team building, 69 percent had added staff, 67 percent had gone through some form of reorganization, 37 percent had created a rainy day reserve fund, 31 percent had tried to enhance staff diversity, and 17 percent had created a fund to support new ideas.

—Among the 85 percent who said their organization had worked on internal systems, 80 percent had adopted new information technology, 75 percent had done some kind of staff training, 62 percent had upgraded their accounting system, 60 percent had worked on program evaluation, 52 percent had engaged in organizational assessment, 48 percent had worked on outcomes measurement, and 39 percent had made changes to their personnel system.

—Finally, among the 77 percent who said their organization had worked on leadership, 80 percent had engaged in board development, 67 percent had worked on greater delegation of responsibility for routine decisions, 63 percent had worked on leadership development, 45 percent had dealt with a change in leadership, and 27 percent had conducted some form of succession planning.

When the numbers are added up, the 318 organizations had undertaken an average of ten capacity-building efforts over the past five years: 70 percent had engaged in collaboration, 68 percent had used new information technology, 64 percent had conducted staff training, 63 percent had done team building, 62 percent had undertaken board development, 59 percent had reorganized, 59 percent had added staff, 58 percent had done strategic planning, 57 percent had addressed media relations, 53 percent had improved their accounting system, and 51 had undertaken program evaluation.

The Impact of Organizational Age and Size

Just as organizational age and size shape employee attitudes, they also influence the direction of capacity building. Although there were simply

T A B L E 3 - 1 . Capacity-Building History, by Age and Size of the Organization
Percent of respondents

Activities undertaken over the past five years	Fifteen years old or less	At least fifteen years old	
		Less than $2 million in revenues	More than $2 million in revenues
To improve external relations			
Collaboration	95	84	84
Mergers	5	8	17
Strategic planning	77	73	69
Fund-raising	64	63	66
Media relations	48	65	65
To improve internal structure			
Reorganization	65	60	81
Team building	73	68	81
Adding staff	78	67	65
Staff diversity	39	22	38
Rainy day fund	35	36	41
Fund for new ideas	27	13	18
To improve leadership			
Board development	86	83	76
Leadership development	57	56	73
Succession planning	31	22	34
Change in leadership	51	48	44
Greater delegation	69	60	75
To improve management systems			
Information technology	71	79	86
Accounting systems	73	59	61
Personnel system	35	30	50
Staff training	77	66	85
Evaluation	58	52	71
Organizational assessment	62	53	49
Outcomes measurement	52	40	56
Sample size	62	118	115

Source: Internet survey of 318 nonprofits completed in 2003.

too few young, small organizations in the capacity-building survey to create the exact age and size measures I use in the employee analysis (tables 2-2 and 2-3), the measures are close enough to confirm the impact of organizational demography on capacity-building histories. Younger organizations do choose different activities than their older peers, while larger organizations do choose different interventions than smaller ones. As table 3-1 shows, the combination of age and size poses a number of tough questions for donors, boards, and executive directors, not the least of which is whether some organizations should continue to exist at all.

Looking at statistically significant differences based on the underlying sample sizes, younger organizations are significantly more likely than older organizations of any size to embrace collaboration and organizational assessment and less likely to undertake media relations, reorganization, team building, leadership development, new information technology, and changes in their personnel system. Younger organizations behave like the more agile, yet naive organizations they are. They adopt capacity-building approaches that build their influence through collaboration and outcomes measurement but show less interest in media relations and new information technology, either because they do not recognize the need or do not have the funding.

In turn, older, larger organizations are more likely than smaller or younger organizations to embrace mergers, reorganization, team building, leadership development, changes in their personnel systems, and evaluation. They are also more likely than their older, smaller peers to focus on greater delegation of routine authority, changes in their personnel system, staff training, and program evaluation. In sum, older, larger organizations behave like weight-conscious organizations: they adopt capacity-building approaches designed to counter bureaucratic encrustation.

Finally, older, smaller organizations are less likely than either younger organizations or their larger peers to focus on staff diversity and outcomes measurement. There appears to be an organizational "middle age" marked by little upward growth in budget and a significantly lower engagement in program evaluation and outcomes measurement. Unlike their younger peers, who are working to get larger, and their larger brethren, who are seeking to act smaller, these older, smaller organizations might ask themselves whether it is time to grow, quit, or merge. If they are to stay in this awkward middle age, they should do so by choice, not inertia.

The Impact of Growth and Decline

Organizational age and size obviously change over time—organizations get older every day and often grow or contract with opportunities and crisis. The question is whether growth and decline produce different histories of capacity building. Table 3-2 shows the patterns.

Growth provides a mix of both opportunity and incentive. It generates the resources to invest in new technology, hire more staff, create rainy

TABLE 3-2. Capacity-Building History, by Growth of the Organization's Budget
Percent of respondents

Activities undertaken over the past five years	Great deal of growth	Some growth	No change	Some or great decline
To improve external relations				
Collaboration	87	86	81	82
Mergers	13	9	8	13
Strategic planning	76	72	81	59
Fund-raising	76	61	69	59
Media relations	63	57	69	67
To improve internal structure				
Reorganization	71	63	61	88
Team building	82	71	61	69
Adding staff	81	71	57	44
Staff diversity	44	31	13	16
Rainy day fund	46	35	22	41
Fund for new ideas	17	19	9	16
To improve leadership				
Board development	28	47	9	14
Leadership development	68	68	41	55
Succession planning	28	32	18	15
Change in leadership	24	51	9	14
Greater delegation	78	70	55	45
To improve internal management systems				
Information technology	86	82	71	66
Accounting systems	60	59	71	72
Personnel system	44	31	42	63
Staff training	84	74	71	69
Evaluation	62	58	71	59
Organizational assessment	56	47	63	53
Outcomes measurement	59	40	54	50
Sample size	87	167	27	46

Source: Internet survey of 318 nonprofits completed in 2003.

day and idea-investment funds, enter into mergers, and place greater focus on staff diversity. At the same time, growth generates a greater focus on succession planning, outcomes measurement, and evaluation.

In turn, decline produces a mix of need and shortage. In theory, declining organizations should invest more in strategic planning and fund-raising, but they may not have the resources. In theory again, they should put more energy into board development and consider changes in leadership, but they may be unable to attract talent in desperate times. At least compared with their peers, declining organizations put a greater emphasis on reorganization, new accounting systems, and personnel systems, all of which can help to restore momentum toward growth.

The task for donors, boards, and executive directors is to determine what causes what. Does growth yield the resources for new technology, or does new technology produce the capacity for growth? Does decline produce the pressure for reorganization, or does reorganization sow the seeds of decline? And what explains the drive for collaboration across all conditions?

The answer involves a mix of cause and effect. Growth creates resources for organizational capacity, which creates opportunity for growth, which creates greater demand for organizational capacity. Nevertheless, there may be some order here and there. As Peter Frumkin and Mark Kim argue, for example, the best predictor of whether a nonprofit grows is how much it spends on fund-raising, not how well it reduces its administrative costs. According to their analysis of eleven years of growth and decline in a sample of 2,359 nonprofits, "Strategic positioning through the aggressive communication of mission is a more potent driver of contributions than maintaining efficient operations. We conclude therefore that the new literature on bottom-line nonprofit management may be giving practitioners useful tools for tightening their fee-based operations, but it does not appear to be helping nonprofits attract the contributions that remain essential to the ability of many organizations to carry out their charitable missions."[19] When they use the term strategic positioning, however, they actually mean the amount spent on fund-raising. Whether the actual fund-raising truly reflects strategic position is anyone's guess.

Even here, nonprofits cannot ignore the link between organizational capacity and strategic positioning. As the executive director of a summer music festival noted, "Our technology change has brought us into the twenty-first century—I mean we had a tower unit that we were using as our server and we traveled with during the summer and had ulcers hooking everything up at our off-site location. We just had visions of losing our database, you know, everything. Now everyone is on the same operating system and has the same programs on their computer. So it really has improved our capabilities for communication." As she noted, the festival could not have implemented its new fund-raising plan without the new technology.

In short, organizational context is an important consideration in choosing a capacity-building approach. Moreover, nonprofits can produce miracles with relatively weak systems. The challenge is always to sustain the miracles.

A Sample of Examples

Although the following pages treat capacity building as a discrete activity, many executive directors view organizational improvement as a sum greater than the individual efforts. My colleague Elizabeth Hubbard summarizes her long follow-up interviews with eighteen of the 318 original respondents: "Many people had trouble thinking about capacity building as a discrete activity—it's simply part of leading an organization, it's 'what we always do.' When asked to give examples of what they've done, some would say that they really haven't done anything new lately because they've been too busy with their strategic planning process, new database installation, or recent capital campaign."[20]

Consider how the executive director of the New Hampshire family services program described his organization's effort to create a team management structure. "It was very frightening at the time because of the organizational culture. One of the good parts about being an old organization is that there's a lot of culture and precedence. But that meant we had the whole structure to convince, so it was very frightening, fairly difficult to initiate."

Moreover, *how* the organization pursued the change was just as important as *what* it wanted to do: "First, you can't over-communicate with board or staff, in small or large groups, face to face. You can't give them a one-page description, an elevator speech. I would never do a reorganization that was top down, not involved with the troops. I'm not saying that I'd give over my responsibility to any level of staff, but I would involve them in the discussion and the early thinking and the 'working-through' process. All of that takes time and emotional energy, and it's expensive. If you have the resources, outside consultants can be very useful. Usually, that allows you to be a part of the process and not the manager, to say nothing of being able to blame the consultants if it goes wrong."

The longer interviews showed just how deep some of the efforts were. As we see later in this chapter, one thing leads to another and another and another. Sometimes, the chain flows logically from one effort to another. This is certainly how the executive director of a Kansas-based program for the developmentally disabled described the impact of her agency's quality program:

> In the past year we have really focused on additional systems to monitor all of our potential areas of risk on a quarterly basis, and I mean we've spent about a year and a half fully developing it. Now it's a function, and our management team reviews and monitors the reports and develops responses and communicates them to the staff. We want to do things right, and if somebody does something wrong, we're going to investigate it.
>
> We have also developed a kind of crisis communication plan so that we have a team in place if we have a situation where we need to communicate not only to staff but to parents and the media. And from that we developed an emergency response team. We have a strong safety committee that manages a lot of the day-to-day issues, but the emergency response team goes a bit further in managing an emergency, whether it be a fire, the weather, some kind of attack, a spill, or whatever. And we have another location set up if we need to move.

Obviously, this organization could not build such sophisticated risk management without other organizational basics, not to mention enough money to build a strong system. But the effort also involved agility. As the executive director explained, "I always tell my staff that we have to be like a basketball team, always on our toes, and we want to have good, sound systems, but we never want to be so entrenched in what we're doing that we can't adjust to things. We don't want to be a big ship that can't turn."

Moreover, in spite of its healthy budget, the organization had made its share of tough decisions over the years: "Communicating to staff is really key so they know that information is not being withheld from them. A year ago right now, we were figuring out how we could cut $200,000 from our budget because of the cuts we were going to take on the basic rates for the services we provide." Earlier capacity building gave the board and executive director the data to make the decision.

Other organizations in the sample had similar experiences. What started out as a website project soon morphed into a personnel review; what started out as a fund-raising plan evolved into the search for a new leader; what started out as a strategic plan eventually became a template for downsizing in tough times. This was certainly the case with a child abuse program in Denver. According to the executive director of the $600,000 program, one thing led to another almost immediately:

> The thought was that the strategic plan would cover three years, from 2002 to 2005. The program committee, our program director, and I came up with recommendations about how we wanted to enhance or improve our home visitation program, which is our core program, and the same with our secondary program. We had just finished when we found out that we were going to lose about 30 percent of our funding.
>
> So this idea about maybe growing and enhancing programs came to an abrupt stop. The strategic plan butted up against the financial realities of the organization. And we made a very tough, but good, decision to discontinue our secondary program at that point. That was not an easy decision to make, but we had good core information to make the decision. We had already looked hard at the program and had already decided that the program really needed a renovation.
>
> So when the money issue came to the entire agency, the decision to discontinue that program made a lot of sense. It was still very, very tough, but to know that it came from a strategic planning process was really a good thing. I absolutely know we would have come to the same decision, but I think the strategic planning process made it more objective. It made it clearer. We had already made the decision independent of the money.

As these two excerpts show, capacity building often enables further capacity building. The effect may not show up in the financial statements, but it is real nonetheless. Indeed, the vast majority of respondents said that capacity building showed them areas they needed to improve.

318 Examples

Organizational improvement may produce a sum greater than the parts, but there are good reasons for studying discrete examples of capacity building nonetheless. Not only does focusing on discrete examples permit specific questions about the who, what, where, when, why, and how of real efforts; it also is a particularly useful way to ask which kinds of capacity building produce results.

The rest of this chapter is built around the 318 discrete improvement efforts identified in the capacity-building survey. After completing the inventory of past activity, respondents were asked to think of the improvement effort they knew best and to describe it in a sentence or two. Almost by definition, the one effort an executive director knew best was also the most important, recent, or extensive.

The 318 efforts demonstrate the remarkable range of what nonprofits have been doing lately to improve performance. Some efforts involved quick changes such as filling an executive vacancy, cutting staff, or reorganizing an office, while others involved longer-term efforts to launch new programs, import new technologies, or change organizational culture; some were tightly focused on a specific problem such as a sluggish website, while others were part of sweeping reform; and some were urgent, crisis driven, while others moved at a more measured pace.

—35 percent described an effort to strengthen external relationships. One respondent described a "collaboration with a local opera company to improve artistic product for both organizations," another focused on "strategic and annual planning that requires management and staff to focus on the needs and opportunities of the organization in a climate in which funding dropped sharply," and others emphasized a range of activities, including implementation of "a rolling three-year strategic planning process that includes stakeholders such as donors, clients, local community leaders, and business representatives," diversification of "our funding base by educating ourselves and developing and executing an annual donor appeal," and "doing a lot more fund-raising and public relations by reestablishing our annual fund-raising walk, which we hadn't done in three years or so, and trying to be more of a presence at community events." Still other respondents focused on improving external relationships through research such as "hiring a good ad agency, doing a detailed analysis of our clients to identify who they were and how to market to that group, developing a single image, look, and feel to our organization," "using audience-center research and staff experience to redesign major programs, while participating in a national pilot-program for performance measurement and management, and using brainstorming and priority assessment to establish organization-wide goals," and "moving to a new location with enough space to do what we wanted."

—18 percent focused on an effort to improve internal structure. One respondent described a "merger with another nonprofit that would be able to provide a stronger, more comprehensive infrastructure," and another talked about reorganizing "the leadership staff to eliminate the deputy director's position and create two new positions, development director and program director." Still others focused on undertaking "major internal restructuring (our organization was on the brink of bankruptcy seven years ago) and many changes in services and programs," restructuring the "entire 'on-floor' operations, including staff in education, visitor services, admissions, theater, and gift shop," "setting a priority that all staff are important, have a right to be respected for their contributions, want to learn and grow, and be recognized for doing so," hiring "a management 'mentor' to take a team approach and put it into practice with our administrative staff so they could regularly solve problems for and with each other and understand the 'big picture,'" emphasizing "teamwork! teamwork! teamwork!" "letting go of lesser-performing staff members, which sent a powerful message through the ranks," developing "a voluntary separation program to reduce the salary base and bring it into alignment with net tuition revenue," "cutting staff and reorganizing responsibilities," outsourcing "our mailing programs to cut costs," and "establishing a rainy day fund by setting aside $100,000 over a five-year period."

—16 percent concentrated on an effort to strengthen leadership and governance. One respondent talked about the organization's effort to "recruit a new board of fourteen after the previous board had drifted away or been serving too long," and another focused on an initiative to "revamp our governance structure, reduce board size, implement an attendance policy, and conduct organizational assessment." Others highlighted leadership and governance initiatives, including "devoting twenty minutes per board meeting to the board's role, fund-raising involvement, and staff development, all of which has led to a new vision, a focused approach to budgeting and program development," undertaking "leadership development for the top thirty managers in the organization by hiring consultants to assess and train managers in planning and problem solving," replacing "the president and CEO and 95 percent of the staff," moving "the board from day-to-day management to oversight after hiring new staff leadership," "hiring an executive director with business management experience," replacing "the former director who had a terrible relationship with the staff," implementing a "changed management philosophy and style," and undertaking an effort to "reduce staff turnover by involving staff in every level of decisionmaking."

—24 percent identified an effort to enhance management systems. Many respondents focused on technology, for example. One talked about an effort to "improve technology use, increasing information management and accuracy," another, about "improving our database and tracking program performance," and still others, about adopting "updated technology, including better e-mail, voice mail, computers, and printers," creating "a greater online presence," and "totally revolutionizing the information technology, including engaging outside consultants to evaluate existing staff, hardware, software, training, processes, and knowledge base and eliminating the Information Resources Department." Other respondents talked about new management and budget initiatives, including a first-ever effort to analyze "staff time and overhead expenses and allocate costs to specific programs, then conducting a financial analysis to determine which programs were 'paying their way' and which were operating at a loss," hiring "a highly trained bookkeeper," adopting "hiring standards to identify responsible employees," evaluating "job descriptions and adding more flexibility, taking into consideration each staff member's strengths and weaknesses," conducting "individualized training," undertaking "an extensive internal audit, hiring a management expert and colleague, conducting 360 degree reviews, committing ourselves to a written strategic plan," "opening the organization to greater scrutiny and accountability, replacing a majority of board members," "asking each program director to develop time lines with measurable deliverables, including goals and objectives that are related to organizational goals we set as a team," "putting an outcomes-based measurement in place for all programs, including internal and external validation, pre-post testing, time-series *analysis*, quarterly reports on everything," "hiring a continuous quality improvement director," and "implementing a new scheduling process, which allowed us to increase capacity by 22 percent without adding staff."

Strategic planning accounted for 10 percent of the 318 efforts, followed by reorganization and changes in leadership (7 percent each), media relations and program redesign (6 percent each), new technology (5 percent), fund-raising and additional staffing (4 percent each), and board development, outcomes management, and general mentions of overall process improvement (4 percent each). While 4 percent of the respondents typed in such broad efforts that they could not be placed in any single category, 3 percent did not give enough detail. There is no doubt that prayer is a powerful intervention for many organizations, but it is rather difficult to code.

The Depth of Engagement

Before turning to further details on how these 318 efforts were implemented, it is useful to note two quick insights about the list. First, three-quarters of the improvement efforts were still under way at the time of the survey, and slightly more than half had lasted at least a year. Either nonprofit executives think mostly in the present tense or most improvements take time or both. New technologies were the most likely to be both ongoing and long term, while reorganizations and leadership changes were more likely to be ongoing but short term. At least for these respondents, capacity building did not end with a strategic plan, a new executive director, a merger agreement, or a technology purchase. It certainly did not end with a new collaboration; collaboration can hardly succeed on the first day it begins.

Second, and more important, the list itself supports the link between organizational capacity and program performance. Given the opportunity to pick any effort that their organization had made to improve its performance, whether successful or unsuccessful, almost all of the respondents focused on efforts to improve organizational capacity, not program goals. Although these respondents were just as likely as other nonprofit executives to agree that an organization can be very effective in achieving its program goals and not be well managed, their organizations had clearly been working to create the conditions for sustainable program success.

The longer interviews revealed just how concerned respondents were about strengthening organizational performance. Some spoke of their own commitment to a particular style of management. As the executive director of a Kentucky family center explained, "Unless the organization reaches out and strengthens its programs, it will not survive. I am of the school that without collaboration—and in my part of the country there are a lot of people who refuse to collaborate because of the numbers game—you will not survive either. I collaborate with anybody who comes in my door and has a program or needs a program that we can work with. In my mind, collaboration is going to be my key to improving services."

Others spoke of an awakening about performance, for example. As the executive director of a Massachusetts drug treatment program remembered, "It was probably five years ago when the senior management team of the organization was doing our annual retreat and started to look at the amount and quality of services we were delivering. We were all convinced that we were delivering quality services but actually had no data to prove it. And then we got into a pretty frank discussion about the nature of funding and how we had built this continuum of care that was held together by threads." The head of an Arizona affordable-housing agency echoed the point: "I think nonprofits are waking up now and saying, 'We've got to do business differently; we've got to become much more customer oriented; we've got to work with other people because there just aren't enough resources out there to do it yourself.' When you go it alone, you start to stretch yourself too far."

Still others spoke of their own value system and personal beliefs. My favorite interview on this involved the head of a Baltimore arts organization that had adopted outcomes management: "I am an old Quaker. My dad was a union organizer. My mother was a community organizer. And you have to bring what you are in a leadership position. And you do bring your values. Our motto is, 'If the system isn't working, find a better system.' No shame, no blame—sometimes things work, and sometimes they don't."

The question is how this personal commitment to making things work translates into outcomes measurement. For the arts organization, part of the incentive came from the federal government's National Endowment for the Arts, which put a great deal of money into organizational development during the Clinton administration. Part came from external pressure: "There are funders who are requiring it, sometimes without knowing what they are requiring." Part came from the executive director's own view of how life works: "You try to be more effective, which is the only reason for doing it. I can't see another reason. I think it is just so much a part of what we do that it would seem weird if we didn't do it."

There are those who thought it could not be done, however. "I do believe arts organizations and others are reluctant to try to quantify or evaluate the magic of creativity. They think it can't possibly be done. But honestly, it is just observation. You have a kid who picks up his pot and is showing it to other kids. He wants to take it home. He doesn't want to leave. He is hugging his little pot. You have to observe that stuff. And so we end up having little sheets of check-offs for our evaluations and will do a little training on how to do this. And that has a side benefit, too, in that it gets them to see some other teaching methods."

First Steps toward Improvement

At least for the 318 respondents who participated in the survey, capacity building was almost always defined in terms of organizational, not program, improvement. This does not mean that program improvement is not a form of capacity building, however. The 318 respondents concentrated on organizational improvement in part because the survey itself focused largely on organizational improvement. Moreover, respondents were asked to identify the effort they knew best only after they had completed the long inventory of organizational improvements described in table 3-1. As such, they were primed to identify organizational, not program, improvement.

Furthermore, executive directors may have focused on organizational improvement because that is where they added value to the organization. As Richard Daft explains, programmatic innovations (which he labels as "technical") are often sparked at or near the "core" activity of the organization—for example, in the classroom, clinic, theater, or food center—while administrative innovations tend to come from the top. As Daft writes, "Administrative ideas would originate near the top of the organizational hierarchy and trickle down; technical innovations would originate near the bottom of the hierarchy and trickle up. Innovative ideas follow different paths from conception to approval and implementation."[21]

The two types of innovation are closely related, however. Program innovations often require administrative reforms, while administrative reforms often provoke program innovations. Thus all twenty-one program efforts on the capacity-building list either prompted or responded to organizational improvement. Some of the organizational changes were simple—for example, starting a new "Kid's Café" to help low-income children required more staff and food; adding mental health services to a health clinic required a different kind of oversight, a different billing process, and different staff; creating a new dance program required audience research and new outreach.

Other changes were far more complex. Consider the new tele-medicine program implemented at a visiting-nurse program that participated in the survey. According to the executive director, the innovation reflected both internal and external pressures. "Improving organizational performance has always been a priority issue—that we continuously improve patient care and improve the efficiency of our processes. An external impetus is the fact that Medicare is now publicly reporting agency outcomes. . . . I think that there are some indications that in the future Medicare is going to go toward pay for performance."

Moreover, the tele-medicine system cannot be viewed as an innovation unto itself. The system is built around an in-home unit that transmits key data such as blood pressure, temperature, weight, glucose, and so forth to a central processor, which can be monitored for warning signs. "This thing speaks a patient's language," the executive director explained. "Every day at a given time, the monitor goes on and says, 'Good morning, now it is time to check your vital signs. . . . Then it asks a series of questions that we have programmed from a library of questions available to us."

Although it seems simple enough, the tele-medicine system produces a host of secondary, or stitch, effects, not the least of which are raw data on patient performance. As the executive director said, "We are telling people that these devices will do nothing when they are delivered. All you have is equipment in boxes that you have to make work. You have to be enthusiastic from the top down. You have to sell that program and keep it alive. For whatever reason, people think the magic happens when the monitors go in the house and that visits will go down. But they don't go down unless you make them go down."

Patients also change. "If they see their blood pressure is up, they want us to run out and check. And we say no. You can have the patient transmit anytime, so why do you need to run out to recheck a blood pressure. You have a $7,500 piece of equipment that can accurately take the patient's pressure. That is what happens if you don't manage the program. In implementing point-of-care devices, equipment doesn't fail, management does." As she noted, "Our agency stopped offering pediatric services because we were not able to keep pediatric nurses. You can't take care of kids with nurses who are experts in adults. If the referral services find out you are doing that, your credibility is shot. Not to mention that it is not appropriate for the patients."

As the old muffler commercial warned, you can pay us now, or you can pay us later: either nonprofits address the organizational consequences of innovation before and during implementation, or they address them later. Unfortunately, too many nonprofits and their donors jump at the latest program innovation without considering the organizational requirements for success.

The Launch Decision

Whatever their predisposition toward or against capacity building, nonprofits rarely have the time or resources to change for change's sake. Rather, they launch most capacity-building efforts to address a specific problem, opportunity, challenge, or crisis. As one of the executive directors remembered, "I found a problem every time I opened the closet door; every time."

In some cases, the decision to launch a capacity-building effort reflects an external event such as new regulations, a slip in public visibility, or growing demand for services. For a Toledo museum, for example, a new media strategy came from declining coverage. As the executive director explained, "We realized that we were not giving the media what they needed to do their job. I mean, we were making it difficult for them to do their job. And we especially looked at print media. We started to provide reporters with stuff on CD-ROM, with images, quotes, and news release copy."

For a Massachusetts visiting-nurse program, the focus on outcomes began with Medicare, which imposed new performance reporting requirements in 1997. As the executive director explained, "We were in an industry that did not have any data—agencies tried to improve based on how they felt things were going, but they didn't have anything other than anecdotal evidence. Now we have hard data. Now we can see home care has a value, and it does improve patient life. Now we can see the patient improving from admission to discharge. And we can ask questions like how many patients have difficulty breathing after thirty days in our program. So we now have a measure of where we need to see improvement."

In other cases, the decision to launch an effort involves an internal event such as a funding shortfall, executive turnover, or a system failure of some kind. For a Georgia homeless program, board development followed a long period of stagnation. "When I got here, the agency was in pretty bad shape and was in debt," the executive director remembered. "We were stagnant and just weren't bringing in the extra cash. We became more strategic in our board recruitment. We have categories of people that we know we need and have instituted a lot of little things, including new committees and a formal application process. It is really dramatic when you look at it."

For a Kentucky family center, the search for a new executive director followed a three-year vacancy. "In effect, the agency was being directed by the employees," the new executive director remembered. "My first challenge has been to rebuild the agency's credibility in the area. All of our funding was intact and is still intact due to our employees who firmly, firmly believe in what they do. But I had to win my employees back because they had been without a leader for three years and had been burned by two interim directors."

And for a Baltimore arts organization, the drive for evaluation started with a basic concern about matching expectations with realities. "The most important evaluation is the one that you do before you start. Consider the end before you begin: when everybody is excited about a project, when everybody is thrilled about being hired, when everybody is thrilled to be asked to your board. Just find out why everyone is delighted. And then try to quantify it in some way. And then you get all that expectation stuff out there and get back to them with goals and objectives and strategies as quickly as you can."

Finally, in very rare cases, the decision also reflects an opportunity created by external funding from donors such as the Edna McConnell Clark Foundation, which makes substantial grants to strengthen and expand already effective children and youth organizations. As the executive director of one of the foundation's grantees explained, the $250,000 grant involved much more than program expansion. The grant also came with a free team of consultants from the Bridgespan Group, a Boston-based nonprofit firm. "It was a very intense effort," she said of the organizational assessment that followed. "The team from Bridgespan was down here every week, basically. Once in a while, we'd get a week off and all breathe a sigh of relief, but they were here for the duration. We started off with our theory of change, which was reiterating what we do, how we do it, why we do it, who we're working with, but that was obviously a critical thing to make sure everyone was on the same page about what we're trying to achieve with our programs. Once we did that, it was all about looking at our programming and what we're doing and how we want to improve it, how we want to grow it, what we need to do to bridge those two things."

These explanations are echoed in the broader sample of executive directors. Thus 57 percent of respondents said their organization's improvement effort was prompted by ideas or concerns expressed by the board or staff, 53 percent by increasing demand for services, 30 percent by a particular problem with the organization, 24 percent because of pressure from clients or stakeholders, 22 percent by a crisis or shock to the organization, and 22 percent by available funding to work on organizational development. Another 26 percent involved a mix of open-ended answers that focused on improving performance, government regulations, a commitment to mission, and general good practice.

Whether the impetus comes from inside or outside the organization, improvement efforts are often designed to solve specific problems. As

TABLE 3-3. Capacity-Building Effort, by Impetus for Change
Percent of respondents

Specific activity identified in survey	Crisis or shock	Particular problem	Demand for services	Pressure from clients	Available funding	Ideas from board or staff	Discussion with colleagues
Broad focus							
External relationships	22	20	55	22	21	58	16
Internal structure	33	38	57	19	24	66	22
Leadership	21	42	35	25	19	60	15
Management systems	17	28	64	33	24	50	39
Specific activity							
Strategic planning	16	19	50	19	22	63	6
Media relations	10	15	45	15	20	65	15
New program	26	16	68	21	32	63	26
Reorganization	32	45	50	32	18	59	23
Leadership change	38	76	29	38	14	62	0
New technology	6	29	71	29	35	59	53

Source: Internet survey of 318 nonprofits completed in 2003.

such, the challenge is to fit the solution to the problem. New technology is rarely the answer to a crisis or shock, for example, although a good accounting and fund-raising package can certainly help to prevent one; strategic planning is almost never the product of a discussion with colleagues, who may be commiserating with each other about the intensity of such an effort, but it is a key response to higher demand for services; new programs are rarely the answer to a particular organizational problem or meltdown but often emerge from the board and staff.

Reading each column from top to bottom, table 3-3 shows how nonprofits responded to different events and opportunities. Looking at broad patterns across all 318 efforts in the top half of the table, for example, crises and shocks were more likely to provoke efforts to improve internal structure than management systems, no doubt because the latter is more time-consuming. In contrast, increasing demand for services was more likely to produce efforts to improve internal structure and management than leadership, in part because basic systems create the capacity for expansion or greater efficiency.

Looking at specific efforts in the bottom half of the table, crises and shocks also tended to prompt reorganization and leadership change, again no doubt because they are quick, relatively low-cost responses to emergencies. In contrast, increasing demand tended to produce deeper, more expensive engagements such as media relations, strategic planning, new programs, and new technologies, again in part to prepare the organization for growth. In turn, available funding tended to promote new programs and technology, both of which often demand additional, hard-to-fund investments in organizational basics such as training, as well as a strategic planning process to reconcile the new with the old.

Patterns in Implementation

There is no such thing as an easy capacity-building effort. It is all hard work. When done well, for example, strategic planning is disruptive and disturbing; when done poorly, it still sucks up time, energy, and money. When done well, a nonprofit merger is still one of the most difficult, even painful, efforts in organizational life; when done poorly, it can destroy all of the organizations involved, not to mention sometimes fragile community networks and friendships. Even a simple executive transition can be extraordinarily stressful.

Given the psychic costs of capacity building, one might imagine that most efforts would involve some advance planning, a bit of funding, access to outside resources, engagement with the community, and so forth. Unfortunately, as the following pages show, many nonprofits do not have the resources or time to build capacity by the book. Some move ahead with minimal planning, others without funding, and still others without any contact with the outside world. As we see below, the nonprofit sector has a certain expertise in what I call "do-it-yourself" capacity building.

Planning and Acting

Capacity building was once viewed as a relatively low-cost investment that was best promoted through small grants. Some foundations gave grantees discretionary funding to launch small-scale improvements of their own choosing, while others established formal organizational effectiveness programs with formal application processes. But as a general rule, capacity building was viewed as reactive and small scale.

It is hard to be anything but reactive when an improvement effort is driven by a surprise such as a budget shortfall or a change in leadership. But even under intense pressure, the 318 organizations did a fair amount of planning for their improvement effort. They may have reacted, but they also planned. Thus 70 percent of respondents reported that their organization did a great deal or a fair amount of planning before they began their improvement effort, while just 28 percent said their organization did little planning. The answers are hardly surprising given their organizational histories. In a sense, these organizations never stop thinking about building capacity.

The level of planning did vary with the initial spark for action. Almost by definition, crisis and particular problems such as leadership turnover do not provide much advance warning. Thus 20 percent of the 318 improvement efforts that began with a crisis or shock involved a great deal of planning, while 35 percent involved not too much or nearly none. Similarly, just 21 percent of the efforts that began with a particular problem involved a great deal of planning, while 36 percent involved little or none.

In contrast, 39 percent of the efforts that began with publications or conversations with colleagues involved a great deal of planning, while only 17 percent involved not too much planning and none involved nearly no planning at all. Efforts driven by pressure from clients and increasing demand for services also provided time for advance planning—roughly 30 percent of these efforts involved a great deal of advance planning.

Ironically, only 23 percent of the efforts that were driven by available funding to work on organizational development involved a great deal of planning, while 27 percent involved little or nearly none. Many nonprofits know the drill—a request for proposal arrives, the senior management team meets to decide whether they can respond before the deadline, an idea emerges, and an improvement effort is launched. It is hardly surprising that these efforts produce less satisfying efforts. As we see in the next chapter, efforts that are launched with a great deal of planning are twice as likely as those with not much or nearly no planning to be rated as completely successful in improving organizational management and overall organizational performance.

Expectations about advance planning have clearly changed with the rise of "venture philanthropy," which emerged from the notion that a good idea is only the first step toward riches. As Christine Letts, William Ryan, and Allen Grossman define the term in making the case for venture philanthropy, the venture capital model "is now a comprehensive investment approach that sets clear performance objectives, manages risk through close monitoring and frequent assistance, and plans the next stage of funding well in advance."[22] Applied in the nonprofit world by the Edna McConnell Clark Foundation and others, venture philanthropy involves a very different model of capacity building that is anything but small and brief. Consider how Mario Marino, founder of Venture Philanthropy Partners, described the model:

> Under this model, rather than a charitable foundation writing a one-time check for two or three years to finance a specified program and then moving on, investors would make a substantial, long-term commitment focused exclusively on building capacity. This commitment would last four to six years and total several million dollars. They would seek nonprofit organizations with both great potential and the commitment to tap that potential to significantly improve the services they provide and expand the number of people who receive them. They would insist that focus be placed on a clear mission and on accountable results that demonstrate a social rate of return on their investment. In addition to gifts of equity— the investment—these givers would also share their managerial and technological expertise. They would leverage their network of contacts. They would help organizations empower themselves to achieve their missions instead of trying to redefine them.

Also consider how the $250,000 Edna McConnell Clark Foundation grant worked for a girls organization that participated in the capacity-building survey. Like any astute venture capitalist, Edna McConnell Clark did not just stumble on the organization. As the executive director of the girls organization remembered, "We had already been building up to having a great year when Clark showed up. I mean we were on the Oprah Winfrey show and won an award for being a top poverty fighter in the United States, and with all that came cash, came volunteers, came support. The Clark grant certainly helped a lot, but there were other things already in play."

Also like a venture capitalist, Edna McConnell Clark made an investment for the long term. "We wound up with a two-year plan. The first two years are what we call our implementation plan, and that's really about six different strategies to make sure we have the foundation for the ambitious growth that we want to achieve in the second three years— things like redesigning our curriculum, strengthening our staffing and volunteer structure, increasing the number of our mentor matches, improving and refining logistics around the different sites that we work

TABLE 3-4. Capacity-Building Effort, by Level and Source of Support
Percent of respondents

Specific activity identified in survey	Effort cost less than $25,000	Effort had outside funding	Outside funding covered all or most of expenses[a]	Overall financial resources were not too or not at all adequate
Broad focus				
External relationships	43	34	72	22
Internal structure	45	31	56	29
Leadership	58	23	58	33
Management systems	54	28	72	29
Specific activity				
Strategic planning	76	31	90	19
Media relations	55	20	75	20
New program	38	47	67	32
Reorganization	36	27	78	27
Leadership change	48	29	50	33
New technology	65	35	67	18

Source: Internet survey of 318 nonprofits completed in 2003.
a. Question was asked only of the ninety-six respondents who said their organization had outside funding for the effort.

at. If we just keep our agency as it is now, we'll go broke. We can't afford to run things as we do now. The Clark money does not cover everything, but it certainly gives us a cushion so that we can build momentum around our plan and bring in other supporters."

Much as one can admire, even envy, the good fortune of this particular organization, the vast majority of nonprofits do not yet have access to that kind of investment and the greater likelihood of planning that comes with it. As table 3-4 shows, the vast majority of the 318 efforts involved small amounts of money and little or no outside support. Roughly a sixth did not require any funding, either internal or external, while another quarter cost less than $10,000. A quarter of respondents did not answer the question, however, perhaps because they simply did not know how much their organization's effort actually cost.

The second column in table 3-4 also shows that the vast majority of the 318 efforts were self-funded. Indeed, only 30 percent of the respondents reported that their organization had any outside funding at all for the improvement effort. Even then, the outside funding rarely covered all the cost: only 26 percent of respondents said the outside funding covered all of the costs, 40 percent said most, 30 percent said some, and 4 percent said only a little. When answers to the two questions are combined, less than 10 percent of the 318 efforts were completely funded with outside support.

This does not mean that outside funding is somehow irrelevant to success. Outside funding increases the odds that organizations have enough resources for their improvement effort, but perhaps by not as much as one might imagine. Among respondents who reported that their organization had any outside funding at all for its improvement effort, 79 percent described the financial resources for the effort as either very or somewhat adequate. Among respondents whose organizations had no outside funding of any kind, the percentage was 14 points lower. In turn, respondents in organizations that had very adequate funding were twice as likely as those with not too or not at all adequate funding (32 versus 15 percent) to report that their organization had done a great deal of planning before it launched its improvement effort.

Neither does it mean that venture philanthropists are spending too much money. As the Edna McConnell Clark example suggests, most venture philanthropy grants involve multiple efforts that sum to substantial cost. Whole-organization improvement is obviously much more expensive than sequential single improvement.

Nevertheless, table 3-4 simultaneously lends some support to the old-fashioned small-grant approach, while suggesting that nonprofits often engage in capacity building against the financial odds. Determined organizations seem to find a way to cover the costs, even when substantial improvements are required. Barely a third of the organizations that pursued new technology had outside funding; for example, the vast majority reported that they had adequate funding for the effort, in part because most of the efforts were relatively inexpensive.

The question is not so much where the funding comes from, but whether the resources are adequate to the task. Does it matter that roughly a fifth of the strategic planning efforts, a third of the new programs and organizational assessments, and nearly half of the outcome measurement systems were implemented without adequate funding? The answer is undeniably yes. Having adequate funding, wherever it comes from, makes a very big difference in the ultimate success of organizational improvement.

Participants in Improvement

Capacity building may be a way of thinking, but almost all improvement efforts involve a process of some kind. Strategic planning can

TABLE 3-5. Capacity-Building Effort, by Level of Internal Participation
Percent of respondents

Specific activity identified in survey	Board	Senior staff	Middle management	Frontline staff
Broad focus				
External relationships	39	85	38	34
Internal structure	31	75	24	21
Leadership	42	71	10	10
Management systems	12	78	42	36
Specific activity				
Strategic planning	47	47	28	22
Media relations	30	70	45	30
New program	32	79	37	47
Reorganization	45	73	23	18
Leadership change	43	62	5	5
New technology	12	65	41	24

Source: Internet survey of 318 nonprofits completed in 2003.

involve a tightly formalized time line, mergers can require seemingly end-less negotiation, board development can involve separations, recruitment, and training, while collaboration can run the gamut from minimal con-tact to intricate governance structures. "We used to say we collaborated," the executive director of an Arizona housing program explained, "but that might have meant we got together a couple of hours a month and did something and called that collaboration. That's nothing compared with what we have to do now. We actually have board to board discussions, true understanding of each other's mission; we see what threatens one and doesn't threaten the other; we see the difference between faith-based housing and our program; it's a very humbling experience, really."

Viewed as a process as well as an activity, capacity building can involve a range of participants, from clients to donors. Inclusive though it can be, most of the 318 efforts covered by the survey were driven by the senior staff. Asked to gauge the level of involvement, 79 percent of the respondents said senior staff were involved a great deal, compared with 31 percent who said the same about the board and middle man-agement and 28 percent who said the same of frontline staff. Asked who was the strongest advocate, or champion, of the effort, 57 percent said the executive director, followed by the board (17 percent), the staff as a whole (8 percent), and a senior staff member (6 percent).

As table 3-5 shows, the level of internal participation varied greatly with the specific intervention. Looking again at patterns across all 318 efforts, the board was a modest participant at best in management systems, while middle management and frontline staff were much less engaged in leadership improvement efforts than senior staff. Looking at specific activities, the board was highly engaged in strategic planning, but less involved in media relations or new technology, while middle management and frontline staff were less involved in leadership change, but more involved in new programs and technology.

This does not mean that organizational improvement is a closed process. Half of the respondents said their organization involved members or clients directly in the improvement effort. Moreover, many of the improvement efforts involved some effort to strengthen relationships with constituents. "I've gone to the community and have said, 'If you have a problem, call me,'" said the executive director of an Arizona affordable housing program. "I think being open with them has developed a trust. If they have complaints, I'll listen to them. I may not agree with them, but I won't be disagreeable."

Neither does it mean that improvement is always done without help. Nonprofits can surf the Internet for advice on improvement, read a book or manual for the technical details, attend a workshop or conference, seek the advice of professional colleagues about what to do, seek technical assistance from a management support center such as San Francisco's CompassPoint, or apply for outside funding to support the effort.

Each of these activities requires some connection to the outside world, be it through a modem, a telephone call, a letter to a funder, or a visit to the library or bookstore. The organizations represented in the survey almost certainly have done all of the above and more over the years.

As noted, the organizations varied greatly in their use of outside resources in their improvement efforts. According to the capacity-building survey, 65 percent of the organizations sought advice from professional colleagues, 53 percent received training through a workshop or conference, 50 percent used a book, manual, or other written materials, 42 percent hired a consultant, 30 percent had outside funding, 25 percent used Internet-based resources, and 16 percent received technical assistance from a management support center. When all the resources are combined, 9 percent of the organizations did not make any outside contact at all for their improvement effort, 16 percent made just one contact, 17 percent made two, 23 percent made three, 19 percent made four, and 16 percent made five or more contacts.

The question is why organizations might decide to engage in "do-it-

TABLE 3-6. Capacity-Building Effort, by Number of Outside Resources Used
Percent of respondents

Specific activity identified in survey	Zero or one	Two	Three	Four	Five or more
Broad focus					
External relationships	33	18	25	13	11
Internal structure	26	17	31	10	16
Leadership	27	21	15	23	13
Management systems	12	14	22	32	20
Specific activity					
Strategic planning	28	16	28	15	13
Media relations	40	5	25	10	7
New program	26	21	21	21	11
Reorganization	23	5	50	9	14
Leadership change	33	14	10	33	10
New technology	6	6	29	41	18

Source: Internet survey of 318 nonprofits completed in 2003.

yourself" capacity building. It could be, for example, that some improvement efforts require more outside contact than others. It could also be that organizations go it alone because they are simply too young or small to do otherwise. It could even be that organizations go it alone because they see little value in making contact.

The survey supports all three explanations. As table 3-6 shows, efforts to improve external relationships were almost three times more likely to involve outside contact than efforts to strengthen management systems, perhaps because nonprofits can draw on board or staff expertise. In a similar vein, efforts to improve media relations and design new programs involved less outside contact than pursuing a change in leadership and new technology, both of which require contact with candidates or vendors.

At the same time, younger, smaller nonprofits are less likely to make outside contact than older, larger nonprofits. Although the differences between young and old and between small and large are relatively small, they are statistically significant nonetheless. Older, larger organizations might need outside contact less, but they clearly have more organizational "slack" or free resources to engage.

Finally, outside contact may not produce the intended help. Asked to rate the outside resources their organizations had used, 61 percent of the respondents said their consultants had been very helpful in the improvement effort, compared with 57 percent who said the same about advice from professional colleagues, 44 percent about technical assistance provided by a management support organization, 38 percent about training received through workshops and conferences, 28 percent about books, manuals, and other written materials, and just 21 percent about Internet-based resources. The more diffuse the help, the less helpful the contact.

These results suggest that consultants can bring significant value to the improvement effort, a point buttressed in the longer interviews. "The sooner you can bring in external consultants, the better," the executive director of a Massachusetts drug treatment program recommended. "The sooner we brought them in, the sooner we saw changes. It was in some ways continued fuel for the fire. When we were dragging our feet, a consult could restart the process over and over again."

Even when they described their consultant as very helpful, some respondents were still critical of the expense or process. "He never made any promises and made it clear that this was going to take a long time," one respondent said of her organization's fund-raising consultant. "He never really said, 'Oh, here's your magic wand, and I'll write all your grants.' He just said the same things to the board that I'd been saying all along, but they totally bought it when they paid money to hear it. God, that's irritating."

If the selection process has something to do with eventual impact, it did not show up in the survey. Asked how they selected their organization's consultant, some respondents simply answered that they already knew the consultant. For example, they said, "I would have been reluctant to select anyone that I didn't know because so many consultants did not meet our needs," "It was someone we use on an ongoing basis," and "It was someone we knew who knew someone." Four respondents typed in "word of mouth," and six answered "referral."

Some relied on their board, networks, or funders for input. According to one respondent, "It was a recommendation from a colleague in a sister agency." Another said, "Someone on our board was an employee in a management consulting firm, and the firm's services were given pro bono," and still others said, "We used a company we knew because it had done work for the firm headed by the chairman of our board of trustees" or "We selected from a list provided by the funder." Several also reported that the consultant came with the grant, saying, "We received a grant for a piece of this planning project, and the funder identified the consultant group; the specific 'coach' from the group was identified to fit our group."

Some used a formal review process. For example, they said, "We interviewed consultants for the first stage of our project and hired one who was recommended to us; we used our human resources consultant for the second stage," "We interviewed several consultants and had them provide proposals," "We utilized information from similar organizations ranking individuals and past experience, as well as their knowledge about our agency and mission," and "The executive director talked to others who had used consulting firms and suggested three to the board of directors, and together they interviewed each one and chose the firm to use."

If not quite a random walk, the process for selecting consultants hardly speaks to great deliberation. Much as the Alliance for Nonprofit Management has endeavored to build a national network of consultants, most consulting work is still assigned through informal contacts and networks. It is not clear that an accreditation process or a seal-of-excellence program would improve the quality of consulting, but it might create more confidence in the industry as a whole.

Conclusions

It is one thing to start a capacity-building effort, make contact with the outside world, and engage the right participants and quite another to produce tangible results. Although capacity building can help an organization to identify areas for improvement, provide a sense of direction, and generate long-lasting gains in performance, it can also prove that change is harder to achieve than expected and create great stress for the staff.

More important, capacity building is far from the slam dunk source of improvement that many organizations need. Of the 318 efforts described in the survey, only 14 percent were rated as completely successful in improving the organization's overall performance, 56 percent as mostly successful, and 30 percent as somewhat successful, neither successful nor unsuccessful, somewhat unsuccessful, mostly unsuccessful, or not rated at all. The next chapter asks just what makes an effort "completely successful."

4 | The Case for Capacity Building

However the term is used, capacity building involves an activity such as planning, reorganizing, merging, downsizing, assessing, auditing, installing, training, recruiting, measuring, treating, and so forth. As such, the case for capacity building hinges on finding a positive relationship between the activity and organizational effectiveness, whether measured by short-term outputs such as morale, expertise, productivity, or efficiency or by longer-term outcomes such as higher performance.

There are many methods for building the case, including expensive structured surveys, such as the one on which this chapter is based, which cost more than $250,000. Largely driven by funding constraints, the best work on capacity building involves more limited case studies of the kind that McKinsey and Company uses in its 2001 report *Effective Capacity Building in Nonprofit Organizations*.[1] McKinsey's thirteen case studies include a large range of organizations, from the Nature Conservancy at $780 million in revenues and 3,000 employees to Powerful Schools at $700,000 and fourteen employees. All of the organizations were engaged in some form of capacity building at the time of the McKinsey study, which was funded by Venture Philanthropy Partners. Tasked with exploring the characteristics of successful capacity building, the study provides rich details on the thirteen efforts, which include the merger of the nation's two largest food banks (Second Harvest and Foodchain), City Year's effort to maintain its core identity as it expanded, and the Nature Conservancy's campaign to increase collaboration across its local members.

Consider its brief description of capacity building at Citizen Schools, a Boston-based organization that seeks to expand student learning before and after school. As McKinsey notes, the $1 million expansion was funded by New Profit, a venture philanthropy partnership among individual donors. Working with a private consulting firm, Citizen Schools and New Profit eventually decided to create a "balanced score- card" to track objectives and measures:

> The Scorecard now serves as a tool both for managing the organi-
> zation internally and for managing the relationship with New
> Profit. Even New Profit's funders will only have to pay their
> pledged funds in later years if New Profit fulfills its own Balanced
> Scorecard, which in turn depends on Citizen Schools' Balanced
> Scorecard. The cumulative effect of all these efforts has been to
> create a culture of measurement and accountability throughout
> Citizen Schools. With the performance expectations clearly de-
> fined—and with the organization's financial health linked directly
> to meeting them—everyone affiliated with Citizen Schools comes to
> work knowing exactly what they need to do.

Although the case studies are too diverse to offer much insight on how the capacity building actually worked, there is little doubt that the capac- ity building produced significant gains for each organization, albeit in very different ways. According to the report, the Second Harvest– Foodchain merger positioned the new organization for a sharp increase in social impact by "simultaneously eliminating competition for funds and food donations," City Year's renown for its powerful culture and shared values helped its revenue to grow from $700,000 in 1988 to $25 million today, and the Nature Conservancy's One Conservancy cam- paign helped the vast national organization to "develop new organization- wide initiatives such as Last Great Places, improve the recruiting and retention of top talent, and conduct more coordinated and aggressive fund-raising campaigns."

McKinsey would almost certainly argue that different kinds of capac- ity building produce different kinds of outputs. Whereas mergers might produce savings, scorecards might produce focus. But McKinsey might also argue that there are common outputs across the thirteen cases, including greater focus, tighter measurement, competitive advantage, higher productivity, and so forth.

This chapter describes the characteristics of successful capacity building by asking structured questions about the 318 efforts identified in the capacity-building survey. As the chapter shows, the impact of improvement is more difficult to measure the further one moves from the actual intervention. It is one thing to show that a given activity produced the intended output, but quite another to show that it altered more general organizational capacity, and quite another still to suggest that it had a measurable impact on program performance. Far too many of the respondents had little more than personal observations on which to judge their organization's improvement effort.

Nevertheless, as this chapter also shows, there is good reason to suspect that capacity building does, in fact, produce potentially measurable impacts on program outcomes, whether greater management focus, increased accountability, more thoughtful use of funds, or increased productivity. Although this chapter is based on the subjective success of the 318 improvement efforts introduced in chapter 3, the statistical analysis suggests that capacity building has clear payoffs for organizational success, even at very low cost.

The Logic of Capacity Building

Measuring the impact of capacity building requires a detailed logic chain-within-a-chain for identifying possible effects. At the front end of the logic chain, a capacity-building effort reflects an attempt to improve effectiveness, whether by strengthening external relationships, internal structure, leadership, or internal systems. In turn, it involves a specific activity designed to produce the hoped-for improvement. A nonprofit that wants to improve its relationships with the outside world might work on its media strategy, strengthen its case for funding, launch a new collaboration, or tighten its mission through a traditional SWOT (strengths, weaknesses, opportunities, and threats) analysis, while a nonprofit that wants to strengthen its internal management systems might import new technology, develop a balanced scorecard or other performance measures for the organization as a whole, improve its financial management system, strengthen governance through greater transparency, or raise the overall expertise of the organization through individual, team, or whole-organization training.

This activity should produce measurable short-term organizational outputs. A fund-raising campaign should produce real dollars; a media plan should generate greater understanding, not to mention more coverage; reorganization should produce a new organizational chart; board development should produce more engagement, but not more meddling; a change in leadership should provoke a cascade of internal reactions; investments in new technology should produce the new technology. Many of these outputs will involve gains such as higher revenues, increased productivity, and so forth, but some will involve pains such as increased stress, confusion, and firings.

These capacity-building outputs should affect overall organizational performance, whether by improving organizational management, program impacts, or both. Simply stated, the outputs must eventually find their way to actual program impacts. Some activities such as fund-raising and new program development directly improve program impact, while others work their will by improving overall organizational effectiveness. Increased productivity can produce everything from lower staffing costs to more clients served for the same dollar, while better morale can generate everything from lower staff turnover and higher client satisfaction to increased efficiency. Unfortunately, as the following pages suggest, the linkages between activities, outputs, and outcomes are often anything but clear.

Untangling Activities

Like most logic chains, figure 4-1, which shows a detailed version of the link between capacity-building effort and organizational effectiveness, oversimplifies a cascade of both intended and unintended effects that include even more chains-within-chains. An organization might start a fund-raising campaign and end up with a new technology system; it might install a new technology system and end up with a new leader; it might recruit a new leader and instantly require board development.

Indeed, some efforts such as strategic planning, new programs, a change in leadership, new technologies, and organizational assessment are best viewed as part of a chain-within-a-chain. For example, assessing leads to planning, which leads to reorganizing, which leads to recruiting, which leads to training, which leads to team building, and so forth.

FIGURE 4-1. Linkages between Capacity Building and Capacity

Capacity building	→	Increased organizational capacity	→	Increased organizational effectiveness

Opportunity— for example,	→	Activity— for example,	→	Output— for example,	→	Outcome— for example,
Environment Structure Leadership Systems		Planning Training Recruiting Communicating		Morale Focus Productivity Efficiency		Stewardship Impact Reputation Governance

Moreover, conversations about capacity building can produce almost everything but comparable information about outputs. At least according to the long interviews conducted with eighteen of the 318 respondents, if you have seen one nonprofit capacity-building activity, you have seen one capacity-building activity.

Try to find the productivity or cost savings embedded in the new culture at a Massachusetts treatment program, for example: "We all believed that if we executed this project appropriately we really could change the culture," said the executive director. "People don't throw stones at me anymore when I talk about the work that we do and use the word 'business' in the same sentence. We've got a mission that has incredible value to the community, but when push comes to shove, I always say our checkbook is no different than your personal checkbook at home. The great thing is that someone will throw in an idea, and I'm no longer the only person at the table who says, 'That's great. How would we pay for that?'"

Try to calculate the rate of return from the broad-spectrum reforms at a girls program helped by the Edna McConnell Clark Foundation. "We all have a really clear measurable plan for what we need to accomplish. I think it helped people to manage their workload, manage their staff, and really manage outcomes. And I think it's made it infinitely easier, more interesting at least, to talk to donors about what we've been doing and what we're going to be doing over the next few years. People love it. They say, 'Wow, I wish every organization could have this.' It raises people's interest in what we're doing."

Measuring the "wow" factor is nothing, however, compared with the change in the executive director's own management philosophy: "I don't know if it's a joy or an annoyance to staff to be thinking about the future and how we're organizing things now to make sure we're thinking about all that. I do think that the magnitude of this underlines the value of it to the organization, and I would be more likely to invest more in organizational development in the future than I may have been in the past because I see the value of the end result."

Even when an effort comes with hard data on costs, it can be hard to assign a specific rate of return to the result. Try to come up with a cost-benefit analysis of the new monitoring units at a visiting-nurse program, for example. "The data do show that patients on the monitor are more compliant with their care plan. Because they are treated preemptively, they don't get into trouble. If we see a patient starting to gain weight, we call the patient to ask how he is feeling and call the doctor to say so-and-so gained three pounds overnight. We are collecting the data to try and show that the monitor improves the quality of life, reduces the visits to the emergency rooms, and reduces anxiety because the patient knows somebody is there."

Yet even with good data and clear costs, the approach is still too young to calculate a simple ratio of dollars to savings. As the executive director said, "It kind of wows the doctors when you show them. They still think we are not sophisticated. We had a 'nay-saying' physician, and we put him on a monitor, and he loved it."

Finally, try to estimate the impact of a new Internet-based ticketing system on the artistic enterprise for a Seattle dance company. As the executive director explained, the link between ticket sales and organizational survival is obvious: "If we didn't raise any money, we couldn't do new productions. Our ability to present high quality on stage is directly related to our ability to raise funds to go forward. So I really think of it as a pendulum that swings back and forth between the administrative side and the artistic side."

Organizational survival does not ensure artistic excellence, however. Dance companies can survive forever by offering classics like the "Nutcracker" and "Swan Lake." Thus the question is not whether a ticket system helps to generate revenues, but how it might create greater creativity, imagination, or risk taking, all of which are nearly impossible to measure.

More important, the new ticket system came online just as the company moved into temporary quarters in a vacant hockey arena. "The arena provided a reasonably acceptable experience once the lights went out," the executive director remembered. "But the rest of it was pretty dismal. Hockey arenas are not built with lobbies, you know, just ramps, and they don't have enough restrooms for women. That, plus the fact that we couldn't do all of the bells and whistles because of the stage, created a pretty significant cash flow problem. Our subscriber base dropped by about 30 percent. Now that we've moved into the new hall, people are coming back, but we're still weaker now than we were when we set out on this." Although the new system guaranteed faster sales in the future, it absorbed scarce resources during a very tense moment in organizational time. Try to build that into a rate-of-return assessment.

Exploring Linkages

Even when activities and outputs are relatively clear, it is often difficult to describe the linkage between the two. Invited to provide more detail on how their organization's improvement affected management and performance, respondents offered a remarkable range of linkages among activities, outputs, and outcomes:

—35 percent focused on changes in external relationships. One respondent linked a merger "with another organization" to "increased depth and breadth of services and added administrative capacity to provide a broader array of services and capabilities." Another tied an effort to develop "a single image, look, and feel to our organization" to "state and international recognition for the quality of the marketing campaign and eliminated a scattered approach to marketing." And still others coupled decisions to assign staff "to serve as liaisons to each member government" with "a stronger reputation as the agency that can get the job done—we have been approached by groups and people who would not have normally looked to us for a solution to their problem," to hire "a qualified person for the fund-raising task rather than rely on board members" with "increased community awareness of our services and increased fund-raising success," and to use "audience-centered research and staff experience to redesign major programs" with "new excitement about the organization in the community that has enabled us to attract more media attention, tackle a $3.9 million fund drive ($2.8 already committed), and add several staff positions."

—30 percent focused on improvements to the internal structure of their organization. One respondent linked the restructuring of "entire 'on-floor' operations, including staff in education, visitor services, admissions, theater, and gift shop" to "a reduction in operating expenses without affecting program services to the public." Another tied the creation of a "coordinated administrative structure to encourage greater sharing of resources, ideas, and services" to partnerships with "groups that would not have been willing to partner with our organization in the past." And another coupled recruitment of "college interns from local colleges" with "overall performance within the context of shelter, food, clothing, and advocacy in a rural homeless shelter," thereby attracting "government representatives to explore our operations as a model for other similar shelters around the country." Still others tied a "$1 million cut from the budget without any layoffs and without compromising the quality of our services" to "a workable budget that is definitely streamlined but doable without doing harm to employees or clients—creativity and motivation were highly evident" and the elimination of "a program that was very costly, yet served very few individuals in our core mission" to "ongoing cost savings of $75,000 a year."

—15 percent focused on improved leadership. One respondent linked "a decision to shorten board meetings to make better and more efficient use of the members' time" to "a board that thinks of itself as more professional and more willing to give more time so that we can reach out in coalitions and collaborations with other groups in our state." Another tied the arrival of a new executive director to "new energy in the organization, improved recruitment, financial management, relations with our partner, and staff management" as well as the resolution of "a messy financial situation" and "the opportunity for a senior staff person to advance," while even confirming the "advantages of a change in leadership." Still others coupled the arrival of another new executive director who was "hired to implement the strategic plan for the organization" with "overall productivity and the ability to add projects through cost savings in other areas" and an effort to reduce staff turnover by inviting "staff involvement in every level of organizational decisionmaking" with "improved relationships with a diverse customer base in a win-win effort."

—15 percent focused on changes in internal management systems. One respondent tied the decision to "totally revolutionize the information technology function, including engaging outside consultants to evaluate the existing staff, hardware, software, training, process, and knowledge base" to "staff team building and less divisiveness among staff (that is, the 'we-they' attitude)." Another linked the recruitment of a "new personnel director who knew what she was doing" to "greater morale among the troops—we're one big happy family." Others coupled efforts to "upgrade the caliber of staff" with being "positioned for future program growth" and implementation of a new benefits package with "confidence and cohesion among the staff." For another, creating "standards for every job position that was tied to department and/or clinic productivity" was linked with a new awareness within the organization that "a culture can be changed"; this effort "identified areas of weakness in communication, helped us to put the past behind us and move on, and drove decentralized decisionmaking." For another, investment in staff training "in all facets of the organization" was linked to "three major awards in the past year—everything is running much more smoothly than it did in the past, and organizational effectiveness has improved." Finally, development of an outcomes measurement system following "an extensive internal audit, the hiring of a management expert and colleague, 360 degree reviews, and a commitment to a written strategic plan" was linked to "a greater focus on what we need to do, a level of urgency, and a clear plan of attack and illustrated where we agree and disagree in senior management."

—Finally, 5 percent talked about a range of broader impacts, including domino effects, new strategic objectives, and hidden costs. One respondent tied a new software program "built on a management style that looks to the strengths of the organization's staff" to "newly discovered talents that have continued to be used to make us a more stable and diverse organization," while another linked a less-than-successful cost-cutting effort to "the realization that maximum efficiency has been reached and that further growth in 'the bottom line' can only come through expansion of the fund-raising capability of the organization." Still another coupled "an expansion of middle management designed to improve accountability" with the diversion of "some resources from direct service to clients and an overall small decrease in the effectiveness of our organization to provide quality, innovative services to our clients."

Assessing Success

Just because capacity building can be complex or even confusing does not mean that it cannot be measured. As chapter 3 shows, respondents were perfectly able to describe their organization's improvement effort across a set of common characteristics. Their organizations either had adequate funding for their effort or something less; they reacted to a crisis, increased demand, a particular problem, or some other prompt; they either called in outside help or worked by themselves; and they either engaged the community or did not. Respondents were also quite ready to declare their willingness to engage in another effort to improve their organization's performance—indeed, three-quarters said they were very likely to try another effort, a fifth said they were somewhat likely, and just 2 percent said they were not too likely or not likely at all to try again.

More important for this chapter, respondents were perfectly willing to assess the success, or lack thereof, across the 318 improvement efforts they knew best. They certainly knew whether the effort was still under way or not, for example, and were quite willing to declare failure here and there. They were also willing to provide three different ratings of success:

—14 percent described their organization's effort as completely successful in improving organizational management, 57 percent described it as mostly successful, and 36 percent said it was somewhat successful or less.

—14 percent described the effort as completely successful in improving programmatic impact, 50 percent as mostly successful, and 32 percent as somewhat successful or less.

—Finally, 14 percent described the effort as completely successful in improving overall performance, 56 percent as mostly successful, and 23 percent as somewhat successful or less.

Just because the percentages are nearly identical for each category of impact does not mean that a particular effort was rated the same in all three categories. Indeed, of the forty-five efforts that were described as completely successful in improving overall performance, only twenty-four were also described as completely successful on organizational management and programmatic impact. Conversely, of the seventy-one efforts described as somewhat successful or less, only forty-nine were also described as somewhat successful or less on organizational management and programmatic impact.

More important for the statistical analysis of whether and how capacity building actually works, respondents were quite willing to assess the impact of each effort on everything from morale to public reputation. Asked to work through a structured list of twenty direct and indirect organizational impacts, for example, the executive director of a Massachusetts treatment program said the administrative reforms had a great deal of impact on the focus of management and increased productivity between 10 and 30 percent and strongly agreed that the effort showed his organization the areas it needed to improve.

Given the same list, the executive director of a girls program said the improvement effort had a great deal of impact on the organization's ability to use resources effectively, the focus of management, innovativeness, funding, and client satisfaction and boosted productivity between 10 and 30 percent; she also strongly agreed that the effort showed her organization the areas where it needed to improve and provided a clearer sense of direction, while generating stress for the staff.

Finally, given the same list, the executive director of a visiting-nurse program said the monitoring program had a great deal of impact on morale, innovativeness, and accountability, increased productivity less than 10 percent, and created long-lasting improvements.

As for the dance company, the hockey arena may have been a bust, but the strategic planning that accompanied it produced a host of good, including improving the organization's ability to use resources effectively, improving efficiency and client satisfaction, and increasing productivity more than 30 percent. Nevertheless, the director expressed a strong sense that the change was harder to achieve than expected and created a great deal of stress.

Making Judgments

In an ideal world, the 318 respondents would have based their judgments on objective evidence collected before and after the capacity-building effort, even as they considered alternative explanations such as economic decline, population growth, and the overall contours of service. Even when respondents are given complete anonymity, their assessments will reflect organizational self-interest—after all, success justifies the time, energy, and funding that might have been invested elsewhere, as well as the stress and frustration embedded in most improvement efforts. Moreover, executive directors may have the greatest self-interest in grade inflation, especially if they are products of an improvement effort themselves.

In the real world, however, most nonprofits do not collect systematic performance data. They can tell researchers a great deal about their program inputs, such as funding, staffing, and square footage, and about their program activities, such as number of clients served, cases closed, and subscriptions sold, but often have little or no data on the actual impact of their work. Although the nonprofit sector is making progress toward better measurement, the rest of this chapter is based entirely on subjective ratings of how the 318 efforts affected a range of organizational outcomes.

Despite the obvious self-interest embedded in these ratings, a substantial minority of the 318 organizations represented in the survey had at least some evidence on which to base their judgments of success. Asked what her organization might do in the future to expand service, the executive director of a visiting-nurse program talked about the costs and benefits of monitoring asthmatics: "We are going through the same decisionmaking process we used in cardiac care and wound care. We have the availability to monitor asthmatics, but we need to ask if that will be of value to physicians. Is it something they are going to trust? Can asthmatics do the monitoring on their own without this equipment? We are looking at all that and starting to meet with the pulmonologists to talk to them. If it all looks good, we have to start getting the expertise in-house."

Unfortunately, the majority of organizations may have nothing but hunch and intuition on which to base their assessments. Only 11 percent of the 318 respondents said they based their assessment of their organization's effort on a formal evaluation, while just 29 percent said they drew on objective evidence. The rest of the respondents (57 percent) based their judgment on personal assessments, which appear to be based more on soft impressions such as "a greater sense of accountability," "a move from 'the way we do things' to 'let's decide the best way to do this,'" "a stronger sense of competitiveness," "better use of agency resources," "greater visibility in the community," "cohesion and collaboration," "a strong bottom line," "a surprising increase in the number of organizations that seek us out with ideas for new innovation and collaboration and partnering," and "ownership, team work, and buy-in."[2]

As table 4-1 shows, *how* respondents judged specific efforts depended in part on *what* their organization actually did. Looking at broad focus, judgments about efforts to improve internal structure were less likely than the three other broad efforts to be based on evaluation, but the most likely to rely on objective evidence. In contrast, judgments about efforts to improve leadership and management systems were the least likely to rely on objective evidence and the most likely to depend on personal assessments. Looking at specific efforts with enough examples to provide statistical confidence in side-by-side comparisons, judgments about strategic planning and new programs were the most likely to be

TABLE 4-1. Assessment of Capacity-Building Success, by Method of Evaluation
Percent of respondents

Specific activity identified in survey	Formal evaluation	Objective evidence	Own assessment
Broad focus			
External relationships	13	32	49
Internal structure	8	37	50
Leadership	11	26	63
Management systems	13	23	64
Specific activity			
Strategic planning	21	24	55
Media relations	5	20	70
New program	19	43	33
Reorganization	7	36	55
Leadership change	14	24	63
New technology	10	15	75

Source: Internet survey of 318 nonprofits completed in 2003.

based on formal evaluation, while judgments about media relations, leadership changes, and new technologies were the most likely to depend on personal assessments.

Some of this variation was almost certainly due to funding: organizations that had at least some outside funding were somewhat more likely to use formal evaluation than those that had no outside funding at all: 15 and 9 percent, respectively. Some of the variation reflected problems in finding measures against which to judge success: everyone seems to believe in stronger leadership, but no one seems to know quite how to measure it; investments in new technology have long produced more paradox than proof on rates of return; and the effects of communication are difficult to assess without significant before-and-after indicators. And some involved difficulties in deciding what to measure: reorganization may produce plenty of streamlining but limited measurement targets. What did not matter was whether the given effort was still ongoing: respondents who picked an ongoing effort were just as likely to say they based their judgment on formal evaluation or objective evidence as those who picked a finished effort.

The commitment to evaluation and objective evidence also varied with organizational age and size. As table 4-2 suggests, respondents from younger organizations were only modestly more likely to use formal evaluation to judge success than respondents in older organizations, while respondents in older organizations were significantly more likely to

TABLE 4-2. Assessment of Capacity-Building Success,
by Age and Size of the Organization
Percent of respondents

Age and size	Formal evaluation	Objective evidence	Own assessment
Age			
Less than seven years	14	29	57
Seven to fifteen years	22	19	59
Fifteen to thirty years	9	26	64
More than thirty years	8	36	56
Size			
Less than $500,000	9	25	44
$500,000 to $2 million	14	27	54
$2 million to $10 million	9	36	61
More than $10 million	11	30	59

Source: Internet survey of 318 nonprofits completed in 2003.

use objective evidence. Aging generates trend lines against which to judge impacts, while size may create a certain hubris about the need for evaluation or greater breadth in objective measures.

Whatever the underlying dynamic for using hard versus softer evidence, the choice did affect the ratings of the 318 improvement efforts:

—Respondents who based their assessments on harder evidence were more likely than their peers to rate their organization's effort as completely successful in improving management (19 versus 11 percent), programmatic impact (24 versus 9 percent), and overall performance (25 versus 8 percent).

—Respondents who based their assessments on harder evidence were more likely than their colleagues to report that their organization's effort had a great deal of impact on morale (53 versus 37 percent), their ability to use resources effectively (57 versus 42 percent), the staff's ability to do their job more efficiently (52 versus 34 percent), the focus of management (66 versus 44 percent), innovativeness (48 versus 39 percent), funding (29 versus 19 percent), client satisfaction (46 versus 28 percent), decisionmaking processes (39 versus 36 percent), accountability among management and staff (53 versus 38 percent), and public reputation (44 versus 35 percent).

It is not clear what causes what in these findings. Does hard evidence create greater confidence in giving a higher rating to a given effort, or are organizations that use evaluations and objective evidence already more likely to succeed? Although both explanations are plausible, I believe that high-performing organizations are much more likely to use hard evidence than their poorly performing peers.[3] The more likely it is that an organization already evaluates and measures performance, the more likely it is that the improvement effort will succeed.

As such, a commitment to measurement can be viewed as essential to the "scaffolding" of successful change. Organizations cannot measure, for example, if they do not have at least some level of technological sophistication, some level of strategic insight about how a program might produce outputs or outcomes, some level of organizational interest, and some amount of planning. Thus respondents who said their organization had done a great deal of planning prior to the improvement effort were almost three times more likely than their peers in organizations that had done little or no advance planning (22 versus 8 percent) to have based their judgment of success on formal evaluation. In turn, respondents who said their organization had done little or no planning where significantly more likely than their peers in organizations that had done a great deal of planning (61 versus 41 percent) to have based their judgment on their personal assessment.

Given these patterns, it seems quite reasonable to treat the choice of evidence as an informal measure of a given organization's readiness for change. To the extent that respondents used harder evidence to make their assessments, one can argue, first, that their organization had the capacity to do so and, second, that the capacity almost certainly existed before the improvement effort began.

Defining Success

The first step in making the statistical case for capacity building is to ask just what respondents were thinking when they rated their organization's effort. Answering the question requires at least some effort to break organizational effectiveness into a set of simple outputs that respondents can rate, which requires another attempt to pin down definitions.

Measuring Outputs

Adopting the Packard Foundation's basic definition of organizational effectiveness as "a rich blend of strong management and sound governance that enables an organization to move steadily toward its goals, to adapt to change, and to innovate," respondents were asked whether their organization's improvement effort had a great deal, some, a little, or not much impact on twelve organizational outputs:

1. Morale
2. Ability to use resources effectively
3. Ability to do jobs more efficiently
4. Focus of management
5. Innovativeness of the organization
6. Funding of the organization
7. Client satisfaction
8. Decisionmaking processes
9. Accountability of management and staff
10. Public reputation
11. Efficiency
12. Productivity

Respondents were also asked whether they agreed or disagreed with six general and specific views of what each organization learned from its improvement process:

13. The effort showed the organization where it needed to improve and where it was doing well.
14. The effort showed that it is very hard to find good consultants.
15. Change is very stressful for staff.
16. The effort gave the organization a clearer sense of direction and priorities.
17. The effort led to long-lasting improvements in the organization.
18. Change is harder to achieve than expected.

Finally, respondents were asked how much impact their organization's improvement effort had on two broad outcomes of capacity building:

19. Organizational management
20. Programmatic impact

These twenty measures of output and outcome provide the foundation for each respondent's final assessment of the impact of their organization's improvement effort on overall performance. Thus completely successful efforts were three times more likely than less successful efforts to involve a great deal of impact on morale, three times more likely to involve gains in accountability, and five times more likely to involve boosts in funding and client satisfaction. In fact, it is difficult to find a single output that did not bear some relationship to overall performance.

However, all relationships were not equally strong. At least measured one-on-one, efforts that improved programmatic impact produced the highest ratings of success, followed by efforts that improved organizational management, efficiency, client satisfaction, morale, effectiveness, and the decisionmaking process.

In turn, many of these items were closely related to each other. Indeed, of the 400 possible relationships among the twenty items, nearly half involved a significant correlation, raising a tangle of questions about outputs. Does higher morale lead to effectiveness or vice versa? Does a better reputation produce greater funding or vice versa? Does management focus precede or follow accountability? Does accountability precede or follow client satisfaction? And do improvements in organizational management precede or follow programmatic impacts?

Unfortunately, the sample of 318 improvement efforts was too small to untangle all the causes and effects. Thus it is better to assume that each organization stitched the items together somewhat differently, depending on its particular situation, than to impose some as-yet-unproven logic chain among the twenty items.

Moreover, the purpose of this section of the analysis is to ask what respondents were thinking when they rated the impact of their organization's effort on improving overall performance. The answer can be found in box 4-1, which shows the results of the head-to-head comparison among twenty-two possible definitions of success: whether the effort showed the respondent that (1) change is harder to achieve than expected, (2) it is very hard to find good consultants, (3) change is very stressful for staff, and (4) the organization needed to improve in some areas and was doing well in others; whether the effort (5) gave the organization a clearer sense of direction and priorities and (6) led to long-lasting impacts; the respondent's rating of (7) the effort's impact on employee morale, (8) the organization's ability to use resources effectively, (9) the staff's ability to do their job more efficiently, (10) management focus, (11) innovativeness of the organization, (12) funding, (13) client satisfaction, (14) decisionmaking, (15) accountability among management and staff, and (16) public reputation; the respondent's estimate of the effort's impact on (17) efficiency and (18) productivity; (19) a summed measure of the amount of contact with the outside world the effort involved; the respondent's rating of the effort's success in improving (20) organizational management and (21) program impacts; and (22) the degree to which the respondent's rating of the effort was based on hard or soft evidence.

As the box shows, only four of the twenty-two measures are significant predictors of how respondents defined success. Simply put, successful

> **BOX 4-1.** Definitions of Success in Improving Overall Performance
>
> Four definitions of success are statistically significant:
>
> 1. Effort improved programmatic impact,
> 2. Effort improved organizational management,
> 3. Effort produced long-lasting impacts,
> 4. Effort increased productivity.
>
> Note: The sample size was 318. These results were produced through ordinary least-squares regression of the overall performance ratings in the capacity-building survey. Strength is measured using standardized beta weights, and significance is based on t tests, which indicate the chance that a given result is not the result of random occurrence. The adjusted R^2 for the overall model is 0.477, meaning that the analysis explains roughly 48 percent of the variation in the ratings, a strong result that is significant at the 0.000 level.

capacity building produces program and management impact, increases productivity, and achieves durability.

Box 4-1 is also important for what does not matter to the ratings of overall success. First, much as efficiency might matter to boards, donors, watchdog groups, and regulators, for example, it did not have a significant impact on how respondents rated their organization's improvement effort. Unlike private businesses or government, where efficiency in the form of higher profits or lower costs is honored as an end in itself, efficiency is only a means to an end for most nonprofits.

It is the conversion of savings into program impacts, which are best measured by productivity, that made the big difference in the final ratings. Translated into a variation of the earlier discussion of necessary and sufficient conditions for program impacts, these respondents were clearly saying that an organization can be very efficient and still not achieve program results. At the same time, higher productivity and more program impacts appear to be two sides of the same coin. As such, nonprofit productivity is best measured as doing more for the same amount of money or less.

Morale, management focus, increased funding, client satisfaction, improved decisionmaking, public reputation, stress, organizational self-awareness of the need for improvement, and a clearer sense of direction did not make the list of significant explanations for success. Again, respondents seemed to distinguish between the characteristics that make an effort ultimately worthwhile and all the side benefits that might make it nice. Simply put, if the effort does not change how an organization actually delivers the goods and services, why bother? To rephrase the question asked earlier in the survey, an organization can have very high morale, intense focus, loads of funding, high client satisfaction, and tight decisionmaking and still not achieve its program goals.

Box 4-1 helps to frame the rest of this chapter for those who either fund or lead improvement efforts. At least for these 318 respondents, capacity building was very much about the organization's basic mission. Few appeared to believe in organizational effectiveness as an end in itself: they did not plan for planning's sake, create new programs just to innovate, or change leaders to keep the turnstiles moving.

Rather, much as they might have longed for high-speed Internet access, satisfied employees, and effective teams or want a job description for every position, they considered an improvement effort mostly or completely successful only if it generated long-lasting gains in what the organization delivers. Management improvements were only successful if they generated increased productivity and accountability; program improvements were only useful to the extent that they produced greater results. These organizations did not improve to be pretty or nice; they improved because they believed in the logic chain described earlier in this book.

Evidence of Impact

Much as the 318 executive directors shared a general definition of what constitutes success, their organizations clearly followed many different paths to improvement. Although the vast majority of the organizations represented in the survey had done work in all four areas of improvement, the probabilities that they did everything in the same order are infinitesimal, confirming my belief that "there is no single pathway to excellence." As I wrote in 2002, "There appear to be multiple starting points for improvement, several general strategies for growth, and a menu of characteristics that nonprofits can draw upon as target destinations for building capacity. Nonprofits can achieve and sustain high performance without being practically perfect in every way."[4]

As if to prove the case again, recall that the 318 respondents took very different paths when they were asked to think about the one improvement effort they knew best: 35 percent described an effort to improve external relationships, including collaboration, strategic planning, fundraising, and media relations; 18 percent focused on internal structure, including reorganization, team building, downsizing, and internal communication; 16 percent centered on leadership, including board development, succession planning, a leadership change, and greater delegation of authority; and 24 percent remembered an effort to strengthen management systems, including new technology, accounting and financial management, evaluation, personnel, and outcomes measurement.[5]

As table 4-3 suggests, these efforts produced a variety of impacts, ranging from self-awareness to increased staff morale. Moreover, as appendix A shows, many efforts also produced significant estimated increases in both productivity and efficiency. According to respondents, roughly two-thirds of the 318 efforts generated productivity and efficiency gains of at least 10 percent.

The table offers a variety of insights for nonprofits that are trying to match improvement efforts to specific problems. Within the broad focus of improvement, efforts to address external relationships offered by far the greatest returns for public reputation; no other group of efforts came close. In turn, efforts to address internal structure offered their greatest returns for the ability of staff to do their job effectively; leadership produced the greatest returns for management focus, decisionmaking process, and accountability; and management systems generated their greatest gains in effectiveness and efficiency.

Different efforts also produced very different estimated gains in productivity and efficiency. General efforts to strengthen leadership produced the greatest gains in productivity: 39 percent of the leadership efforts generated estimated productivity gains of more than 30 percent, compared with 29 percent for management systems, 28 percent for structural efforts, and 21 percent for external relationships. Leadership also produced the greatest gains in efficiency: 42 percent of the leadership efforts generated gains in efficiency of more than 30 percent, compared with 33 percent for internal structure, 20 percent for external relationships, and 19 percent for management systems.

Turn next to the relatively short list of specific efforts with enough examples to allow statistical comparison. Within the list, strategic planning had its greatest impact exactly where one would expect: on management focus. Media relations also had an impact where one would expect: on public reputation. So it goes down the list: new programs had the largest effects on client satisfaction and public reputation; reorganization

TABLE 4-3. Output of Capacity Building, by Type of Effort

Percent of respondents identifying the organization's effort as having a great deal of impact on the output

Specific activity identified in survey	Morale	Effectiveness	Efficiency	Focus	Funding	Client satisfaction	Decisionmaking	Accountability	Reputation
Broad focus									
External relationships	44	43	27	46	35	45	25	26	52
Internal structure	47	52	48	55	12	26	38	45	26
Leadership	48	33	46	62	19	19	48	54	33
Management systems	36	55	50	46	12	30	37	53	29
Specific activity									
Strategic planning	53	41	25	72	22	25	47	25	38
Media relations	45	40	20	35	45	50	15	20	70
New program	26	37	37	32	26	74	11	11	63
Reorganization	50	41	41	68	5	18	50	55	27
Leadership change	71	62	71	90	24	33	67	76	38
New technology	29	53	47	18	6	35	24	47	24

Source: Internet survey of 318 nonprofits completed in 2003.

had its biggest impact on management focus, accountability, decision-making, and morale; and new technology worked its will on effectiveness and efficiency.

The largest, and perhaps most surprising, results involved changes in leadership, which affected everything from management focus to accountability, decisionmaking focus, morale, efficiency, and effectiveness. Unlike the other specific interventions, which had impacts exactly where theory and past research would predict, leadership change appeared to cure all that ails nonprofits. It lifted staff morale, improved decisionmaking, and increased both productivity and efficiency: 57 percent of the leadership changes produced efficiency gains of more than 30 percent, followed by new technology (33 percent), while 55 percent generated productivity gains of more than 30 percent, followed by new technology (40 percent).

Table 4-3 offers three simple lessons to nonprofits. First, there is a clear link between certain interventions and their logical results—almost all of the improvement efforts had their greatest impacts exactly where expected. Media relations are not going to solve problems related to efficiency, decisionmaking, and accountability, for example, but they are the "go-to" effort for public reputation; reorganization is not going to do much to increase funding or client satisfaction, but it is among the efforts of choice to improve management focus, improve morale, and increase accountability.

Second, there are obvious trade-offs across the efforts in cost and benefits. Reorganization may yield significant benefits in focus, morale, and accountability but is generally much more disruptive than strategic planning and less likely than media relations and leadership change to have secondary impacts on other beneficial outputs, such as increased funding. Similarly, strategic planning clearly has extraordinary value for producing management focus and staff morale but also has a disruptive, time-consuming quality that creates trade-offs against other improvement strategies.

Third, simply replacing a leader is unlikely to produce all the effects described in table 4-3. In some organizations, it is merely the first step toward a variety of improvement efforts such as planning, reorganizing, collaborating, and so forth. In other organizations, it is the logical con- sequence of earlier improvement efforts that require a different kind of leadership. In still other organizations, it is the natural consequence of the evolution of the organization from one stage of the development cycle to another: the founder wears out or needs to move on, the organization needs a participatory leader to replace the charismatic fundraiser, and so forth.

These findings are echoed in table 4-4, which shows the lessons learned from the 318 efforts. Management systems are the most difficult to change and the most likely to generate concerns about finding consultants, while leadership changes are the preferred path for a clearer sense of direction. There is significant agreement that capacity building showed the 318 organizations areas where they needed to improve and areas where they were doing well.

These lessons were not shared across all organizations, however. Respondents at younger organizations were more likely to say their improvement effort showed that change is harder to achieve than their peers at older, larger organizations; they were also more likely to report that their organization's effort created a greater sense of direction and priorities. But regardless of size and age, most of the 318 organizations experienced the same level of stress, the same frustration, or lack thereof, with finding good consultants, and the same increase in self-awareness.

Given these variations across both outputs and lessons learned, it is not surprising that different kinds of improvement produced different perceptions of overall success. As table 4-5 shows, the activities undertaken varied in their effect on organizational management, program impacts, and overall performance.

The table provides further insight on the match between effort and impact. Efforts to improve internal structure had surprisingly less impact on organizational management than predicted by the research literature, while all four broad areas produced similar improvements in program impact. Once past the broad focus, however, there were important differences among the efforts: media relations, new program development, and leadership had more impact on program than on management, while new technology had a much greater impact on management than on program. As for overall organizational performance, leadership change emerged again as the most powerful intervention for producing gains, with strategic planning and new technology far behind.

There are several possible explanations for the enthusiasm toward leadership change, not the least of which is the fact that many of the respondents who picked leadership change as the effort they knew best were, in fact, the product of the change. Without impugning their

TABLE 4-4. Learning from Capacity Building

Percent of respondents saying that their organization's effort somewhat or strongly affected an area

Specific activity identified in survey	Change is hard to achieve	Change is very stressful for staff	Good consultants are hard to find	Effort showed areas of needed improvement	Effort gave a clearer sense of direction	Effort led to long-lasting improvements
Broad focus						
External relationships	52	43	18	85	65	60
Internal structure	55	43	26	78	55	60
Leadership	50	35	25	87	75	60
Management systems	65	37	30	87	62	55
Specific activity						
Strategic planning	53	53	25	94	78	66
Media relations	40	25	10	75	65	69
New program	53	37	16	79	68	47
Reorganization	50	41	27	77	55	55
Leadership change	48	43	33	81	71	62
New technology	76	41	41	94	53	59

Source: Internet survey of 318 nonprofits completed in 2003.

TABLE 4-5. Outcome of Capacity Building, by Type of Effort
Percent of respondents saying that their organization's effort was completely or
mostly successful in improving an area

Specific activity identified in survey	Management	Program impact	Overall performance
Broad focus			
External relationships	54	63	71
Internal structure	55	69	71
Leadership	77	68	77
Management systems	67	61	68
Specific activity			
Strategic planning	60	54	68
Media relations	40	70	75
New program	37	73	79
Reorganization	64	59	82
Leadership change	57	71	95
New technology	77	41	65

Source: Internet survey of 318 nonprofits completed in 2003.

responses, these respondents had self-interest in seeing the value of leadership change as the tool of choice.

At the same time, however, leadership change almost certainly has much more immediate impacts on organizations than long-term investments, such as new technology or program development. It may well be that a simple change at the top of the organization can boost productivity, raise morale, and improve focus. "At the risk of sounding egotistical," one respondent said of his hiring, "the best move the board made was in replacing the former director, who had a terrible relationship with the staff and was not liked in the community." His organization's public reputation had to get better in part because it could not get worse.

It may also be that leadership change triggers secondary and tertiary improvements. As one respondent wrote of her arrival, "Turnover in the executive director position led to reorganization: pushing decisions, staff management down to the program management level, coupled with strong communication between the executive and program management (weekly meetings) and regular strategic planning." As another described his organization's effort, "The organization replaced the president and CEO and 95 percent of the staff; staff participated in extensive training; the organization built out a website, converted to a new database system, upgraded the software, solicited donations of furniture, and sought in-kind donations." Although the answer was coded as leadership change, it obviously encompassed much more.

Ultimately, many of these organizations did not change the leader so much as the leader's work. Although there is ample evidence that leaders do matter to organizational success, I believe that the measure of an effective leader is not in the individual's tenacity, charisma, endurance, or persuasiveness. As I wrote of the 250 executives interviewed for *Pathways to Nonprofit Excellence*, the measure of an effective leader is "in the leader's ability to drive a sense of mission down through the organization, upward into the board, and outward into the community and to be willing to do whatever it takes to enable the organization to follow that mission effectively." If leadership change is the only way to get that kind of leadership, so be it.

A Brief Note on Productivity and Efficiency

To the extent that the productivity and efficiency gains cited above are remotely accurate, capacity building appears to generate very high rates of return on investment. According to the Internet survey, 78 percent of respondents said that their organization's effort had a great deal or some impact on the staff's ability to do their job efficiently, while 84 percent had a similar impact on their organization's ability to use resources effectively. Asked, in turn, about the actual increase, more than half of these respondents said that their organization's effort had generated a 10–30 percent gain in both productivity and efficiency, while another quarter said the gain was more than 30 percent.

There are several problems with using these estimates to generate a social rate of return on the actual capacity-building efforts identified in the survey. First, many respondents reported no hard evidence on which to rate their organization's overall improvement effort, which suggests that their productivity and efficiency estimates were highly subjective at best. Second, inexpensive improvement efforts generated just as great an impact on productivity and efficiency as more expensive efforts, again suggesting that the estimates were highly subjective. Third, respondents were given fixed choices for making their estimates, which may have sharply reduced the number who would have answered "don't know" if asked to make an estimate on their own. Finally, the estimates included a very high percentage of efforts that were still ongoing at the time of the survey, which raises further questions about their validity.

Even acknowledging these caveats, there is still reason to suggest a high rate of return on investment. Among efforts that were (1) finished at the time of the survey and (2) judged with a formal evaluation or objective evidence, 89 and 82 percent produced estimated productivity and efficiency gains of 10 percent or more, respectively. Although the measurements may be inflated by wording of the question, the responses strongly suggest that there are rates of return to be found in capacity building. The challenge is to develop a valid system for actually calculating and validating the yield.

The Link between History and Success

The 318 organizations represented in the survey had a great deal of practice at capacity building. Recall that the 318 had engaged in ten capacity-building efforts, on average, over the five years preceding the survey. Asked whether they had done anything at all to improve external relationships, internal structure, leadership, or internal systems, all but one of the 318 checked at least one, 12 percent checked two, 25 percent checked three, and 58 percent checked four. Asked next about twenty-three specific capacity-building initiatives, 14 percent checked five or less, 33 percent checked six to ten, 30 percent checked ten to fifteen, and 23 percent checked fifteen or more.

This history of capacity building clearly affects the present. Compare the organizations that had done at least one thing in all four areas of improvement with those that had done at least one thing in two or fewer areas of improvement. Among respondents in the first group of organizations, 68 percent rated their specific improvement effort as completely or somewhat successful in improving management, compared with just 50 percent of respondents in the second group; 65 percent in the first group rated their effort as completely or mostly successful in improving program impacts, compared with 54 percent in the second; and, most important, 76 percent of respondents in the first group rated their effort as completely or mostly successful in improving overall performance, compared with 48 percent in the second.

History also affects everything from why organizations decide to launch an effort to how they proceed. Respondents in the first group of organizations were more likely to report that their effort was undertaken in response to a crisis or shock, increasing demand, or pressure from clients than those in the second, but no more likely to report it as a reaction to a particular problem, available funding, or ideas from board members and staff. Although there was no significant difference in the length or cost of the specific efforts between the two groups, or in their access to outside funding of any kind, respondents in the more experienced organizations were more likely to report that their organization had done a great deal of planning for their effort, had very or somewhat adequate resources overall, and had made more contact with the outside world. They were more likely to involve their board and senior staff and to base their ratings on hard evidence.

As for what worked, respondents in the seasoned group of organizations were more likely than those in the second to say that board leadership, adequate time, funding, and staff commitment were all very important to the success of their effort. Their experience also gave them an edge in lessons learned:

—Just 32 percent of respondents in the first group of organizations agreed that their organization's effort taught them that change is very hard to achieve, compared with 55 percent of respondents in the second group.

—41 percent of the first group strongly agreed that their organization's effort showed them areas where they needed to improve and areas where they were doing well, compared with just 19 percent of the second group.

—40 percent of the first group strongly agreed that the effort gave their organization a clearer sense of direction than before, compared with 27 percent of the second group.

Practice does not lessen stress, however. Among respondents in the more experienced group of organizations, 40 percent said the effort was very stressful for their staff, compared with 27 percent of the less experienced organizations. Nevertheless, these respondents reported that their organization's effort produced greater impacts in every output except one, client satisfaction, which may be more a product of program design or external pressure than anything an organization does by way of organization and management. Most important perhaps, 31 percent of respondents in the more experienced organizations estimated that their effort generated at least a 30 percent gain in productivity, compared with just 11 percent of those in the less experienced organizations.

Unfortunately, I cannot be sure why history has such powerful effects, especially since the survey did not ask respondents to evaluate the success of past efforts. It could be that the experienced organizations simply learn how to do capacity building more effectively: perhaps practice does make perfect. It could also be that they lower their expectations over time: perhaps experience teaches them to lower their thresholds. It could even be that capacity building involves a bit of Russian roulette: perhaps the more experienced organizations simply get lucky or pick the more successful effort from their deeper inventory of past efforts. Finally, it could be that experience is merely a surrogate for size and age: perhaps larger, older organizations simply have the time and money to engage in capacity building.[6]

The available evidence suggests that experience is a great teacher, even when change fails. "Good judgment comes from experience," said the executive director of a now-defunct Minneapolis antipoverty program I interviewed years ago, "but experience often comes from bad judgment." Hence more experienced organizations were far less likely to say that their effort taught them that change is hard to achieve. Change was still stressful for their staff, but there were fewer surprises. Moreover, the more experienced organizations were also more likely to improve the odds of success through measurement, planning, outside contact, and adequate funding.

As for variations on Russian roulette, respondents in the more experienced organizations were only slightly more likely to describe a completed effort than their peers, which suggests that they did not pull a successful past effort out of the inventory to make their organization look better. However, size does have an influence on history: 40 percent of organizations with budgets under $500,000 had done something to improve capacity in all four areas, compared with 59 percent with budgets between $500,000 and $1 million, and 68 percent with budgets between $1 million and $2 million. Age has an influence, too, although through an interaction with size. Of organizations with budgets under $500,000, just 33 percent of organizations fifteen years old or younger had done some form of capacity building in all four areas, compared with 45 percent of those more than thirty years old. Simply put, size and age increase experience or vice versa.

Predicting Success

Nonprofits can enhance the success of their capacity building in a number of ways, not the least of which is to match the right effort with the right problem or opportunity. They can put adequate resources behind the effort, find a good consultant, make contact with the outside world,

spend enough time to succeed, prepare to measure impacts systemati-
cally, and do some advance planning. As one of the respondents I interviewed for *Pathways to Nonprofit Excellence* recommended, "The one
thing is to do your homework, including feasibility studies. We are very,
very careful to tell people that there's no sense in reinventing the wheel.
If someone else is doing something similar to what you want to do, seek
their advice. The people in our industry are very willing and open to giving advice."

Nonprofits can also set realistic expectations for what can and cannot
be accomplished with a single effort, such as strategic planning or reorganization, and how fast the results will emerge. Organizations that
expect too much, too fast will always be disappointed by the snail's pace
of reform. "My first piece of advice would be to take it slow," said
another one of my *Pathways* respondents. "The other piece would be to
hold your enthusiasm and make sure you're reinforcing the administrative side of your organization while you are building the service side. You
really do have to balance it."

Dennis Smith, my New York University colleague, made a similar
argument after assessing several multi-organizational technical assistance
programs supported by foundations such as the Dewitt Wallace Fund.
Organizations need time to understand and appreciate the available
opportunities, time to absorb and institutionalize the practices or skills
introduced by consultants or through training, and time to assess the
impacts.[7]

Ingredients of Success

Much as one can applaud a "take-it-slow" approach or celebrate
advance planning and adequate funding, the 280 respondents who said
their organization's effort was at least somewhat successful in improving
overall performance had their own insights on what mattered most to a
positive result. Given a list of factors that might have affected the success
of their organization's effort, 77 percent of the respondents said that staff
commitment was very important, followed by adequate time (61 percent), effective consultants (53 percent), board leadership (46 percent),
adequate funding (36 percent), community support (23 percent), and
events beyond their control (6 percent). In a sentence, luck has little to
do with success.

Not surprising, funding becomes more important as the cost of
improvement rises. Thus only 11 percent of respondents who said their

organization's effort did not cost a cent also said that adequate funding was very important to success, while 32 percent said that it was not important at all. In contrast, 43 percent of respondents who said their organization's effort cost more than $50,000 also said that adequate funding was very important, and 40 percent said that it was somewhat important.

It is not clear why efforts that do not cost anything would elicit concern about adequate funding. Part of the answer may involve wording of the question. Asked early in the survey to estimate exactly what their effort cost in dollars and in-kind resources, respondents may have focused mostly on the dollar costs. Asked later in the survey about the importance of adequate funding, these same respondents may have defined funding to include time, energy, and other forms of organizational "slack," others may have focused on future costs associated with efforts such as strategic planning and reorganization, and still others may have been thinking about the broader costs to their organization of making the change. Most important perhaps, some respondents may have said that their organization's effort suffered because it was done for nothing.

What is clear is that different efforts are dependent on different resources. As table 4-6 shows, efforts to strengthen external relationships were the most dependent on effective consultants and community support, structural changes were much more dependent on adequate funding, leadership improvement required more board involvement than any other effort, while management systems involved the greatest need for adequate time. Conversely, leadership improvement was the least dependent on adequate time, while management systems were the least dependent on board leadership and community support.

The table also shows considerable variation across the specific efforts. New technology was by far the least dependent on board leadership, no doubt because less than half of new technology involved the board to any significant extent.[8] At the same time, new technology was highly dependent on adequate funding, no doubt because the vast majority of these efforts cost more than $10,000.

Leadership changes were just the opposite of new technology, being highly dependent on board leadership and barely dependent at all on adequate funding. Strategic planning was also highly dependent on board involvement, but more demanding of time and resources, while media relations were intensely dependent on effective consultants and

TABLE 4-6. Elements of Capacity-Building Success

Percent of respondents saying that an element was very important to the overall success of an effort[a]

Specific activity identified in survey	Board leadership	Effective consultants[b]	Adequate funding	Adequate time	Staff commitment	Community support	Events beyond control
Broad focus							
External relationships	56	64	37	61	78	29	4
Internal structure	41	47	43	55	76	22	8
Leadership	57	54	27	52	71	18	6
Management systems	26	44	37	67	81	14	7
Specific activity							
Strategic planning	76	69	41	66	83	17	7
Media relations	41	83	29	41	59	12	0
New program	41	33	35	41	82	35	12
Reorganization	67	67	50	61	78	28	0
Leadership change	67	60	19	48	62	19	5
New technology	24	56	53	71	82	24	12

Source: Internet survey of 318 nonprofits completed in 2003.

a. Asked only of respondents who said their effort was successful (sample size was 280).

b. Asked only of respondents who said their organization had used a consultant (sample size was 120).

new programs were more dependent on community support. Once again, the impacts were just about where one would expect them to be, confirming the intuitive experience of many nonprofits, but providing some firmer evidence nonetheless.

The table also confirms the role of the work force in helping change to succeed. Although strategic planning, new programs, and new technology were the most dependent on staff commitment, all of the efforts required some minimum threshold of support. Media relations cannot succeed, for example, unless the organization "walks the talk," while leadership change is doomed if employees do not accept the choice of leader.

Reasons for Success

There are a thousand reasons why improvement efforts succeed or fail. An organization can find the right leader at the right time, fail in its search, or, worse yet, hire the wrong leader at the wrong time; an organization can pick the right consultant for the right effort, pick the wrong consultant for the wrong effort, or simply go it alone; an organization can recruit the right board member with the right connections for pro bono help, search the seat cushions for enough money to launch the effort, or proceed with no funding at all. In fact, so many things can go wrong that it is sometimes difficult to know what must go right. Is it the funding? The staff commitment? Community involvement? Size of the organization? Slack?

Further statistical analysis of the capacity-building survey provides at least some help sorting through the potential explanations for success. As with all of the advanced analyses presented in this book, one cannot test every possible explanation simultaneously without jeopardizing the validity of the result. Thus box 4-2 summarizes the head-to-head statistical comparison of twenty-six possible explanations of success that were culled from the earlier analyses: the respondent's estimate of his or her organization's (1) age, (2) number of employees, and (3) budget; (4) the respondent's statement that the effort was either completed or still ongoing; the respondent's estimate of (5) how much the effort cost and (6) how long the effort took; the respondent's opinion that the effort was prompted by (7) a crisis or shock, (8) increasing demand for services, (9) pressure from clients or other stakeholders, (10) a particular problem with the organization, (11) availability of funding to work on organizational development, (12) ideas or concerns expressed by the board or

---

BOX 4-2. Predictors of Success in Improving Overall Performance

Six out of twenty-six possible explanations of how respondents rated the overall success of their organization's effort are statistically significant:

1. Effort improved program impacts,

2. Effort improved organizational management,

3. Rating was based on hard evidence,

4. Financial resources were adequate,

5. Organization had a history of capacity building,

6. Effort was prompted by increasing demand for services.

Note: The sample size was 318. These results were produced through ordinary least-squares regression of the overall performance ratings in the capacity-building survey. Strength is measured using standardized beta weights, and significance is based on t tests, which indicate the chance that a given result is not the result of random occurrence. The adjusted R^2 for the overall model is 0.475, meaning that the analysis explains roughly 48 percent of the variation in the ratings, a strong result that is significant at the 0.000 level.

---

staff members, and (13) publications or discussions with professional colleagues; the respondent's assessment of the (14) amount of planning involved in the effort, (15) amount of outside funding, and (16) overall adequacy of the financial resources; the respondent's opinion regarding the amount of (17) board involvement, (18) senior staff involvement, (19) middle-management involvement, (20) frontline staff involvement, and (21) client-member involvement; (22) a summed measure of the amount of contact the effort involved with the outside world; the respondent's rating of the effort's success in improving (23) organizational management and (24) program impacts; (25) the degree to which the respondent's rating of the effort was based on hard or soft evidence; and (26) the respondent's history of past capacity building by the organization. As the box shows, only six of the twenty-six measures are significant predictors of overall success.

Box 4-2 presents the strongest predictors of overall performance among the twenty-six possible explanations. Several groups of explanations were dropped from the head-to-head comparison because they showed little predictive power in preliminary analysis. The overall success of an effort does not vary significantly with the level of participation

---

BOX 4-3. Effect of Removing the Strongest Predictors of Success in Improving Overall Performance

When the two strongest predictors in box 4-2 are removed, six explanations of how respondents rated the overall success of their organization's effort are statistically significant:

1. Financial resources were adequate,

2. Effort was prompted by increasing demand for services,

3. Rating was based on hard evidence,

4. Organization had a history of capacity building,

5. Effort was prompted by a crisis or shock to the organization,

6. Organization had at least some outside funding for the effort.

Note: The sample size was 318. These results were produced through ordinary least-squares regression of the overall performance ratings in the capacity-building survey. Strength is measured using standardized beta weights, and significance is based on t tests, which indicate the chance that a given result is not the result of random occurrence. The adjusted R^2 for the overall model is 0.232, meaning that the analysis explains roughly 23 percent of the variation in the ratings, a result that is nonetheless significant at the 0.000 level.

---

of the board, senior staff, middle management, or frontline employees, for example, or with the engagement of the executive director as the strongest advocate. Nor does overall success vary significantly across the four targets of improvement (external relationships, structure, leadership, or management systems), contact with the outside world, or a decision to act because of a particular problem with the organization, ideas from the staff or board, or discussions with professional colleagues.

This does not mean that these factors are irrelevant throughout the capacity-building chain. Rather, the statistical analysis suggests that they appear to have much more to do with what an organization decides to do by way of improvement than with whether the given effort is actually successful. As already noted, outside contact may be essential for launching an improvement effort involving new technology and might be quite powerful in predicting the success of those specific efforts. Unfortunately, the sample of 318 efforts was simply too small to permit this kind of effort-by-effort analysis.

It is always possible, however, that the top predictors in box 4-2—organizational management and program impacts—are so strong that they hide the underlying relationships between how capacity building occurs and its ultimate impact on overall performance. One way to compensate for the problem is simply to remove these two big statistical "sponges" from the analysis and see which of the twenty-four remaining items are the most powerful predictors of success. As box 4-3 on the previous page shows, six measures rise to significance once the statistical curtains are drawn a bit. However, removing the two big predictors also reduces the overall power of the analysis by more than half.

Just because most of the measures included in the analysis do not rise to statistical significance does not mean they are irrelevant to success. Rather, it either means they are not determinative of success or that there is too little variation across the 318 examples to make a mark in the head-to-head comparisons. The fact that boards and senior executives were so involved in almost all of the 318 efforts means that board and executive involvement cannot help to explain the differences between efforts that were rated as completely, mostly, or somewhat successful. The head-to-head comparisons should be used to identify leverage points that might increase the odds of success, not as a checklist of what is important or not.

Conclusions

Although this is not a how-to book, there are at least four how-to lessons in these findings. First, the cost of any given effort may not be a significant predictor of success, but adequate funding most certainly is. It is the number four predictor of funding in the first head-to-head analysis and the number one predictor in the second. No matter where the money comes from—be it from reserves or outside donors—organizations need to find enough funding to get the capacity built. Having outside funding is clearly not essential for success; otherwise 60 percent of the efforts would have failed. But outside funding can increase the odds that total funding will cross the tipping point for success, particularly for smaller, younger nonprofits and those whose budgets are stable or in decline.

Second, capacity building is not a luxury when it is designed to meet expanding need. To the contrary, capacity building that is prompted by increased demand is the number six predictor of success in the first head-to-head comparison and number two in the second. Although crises and shocks also show up as number six in the second head-to-head comparison, organizations that face one emergency after another can hardly be described as exemplars of sustainable excellence. All those leaky pipes and broken windows may be a sign of deeper problems that demand longer-term solutions.

Third, hard evidence is essential for success. Using hard evidence is the number three predictor of success in both head-to-head analyses. Nonprofits can hardly use objective evidence for capacity building, for example, if they do not use it for anything else; neither can they connect to the community for capacity building if they have no connections in the first place. As such, the commitment to measurement may be an essential first step toward successful capacity building and one of the most important early investments a nonprofit can make.

Fourth, past capacity building clearly affects future success. Having a deeper history of capacity building is the number five predictor in the first head-to-head comparison and number four in the second. Although it is impossible to know how successful these past efforts were, it seems reasonable to suggest that many of these efforts provided the scaffolding for future success. Thus even as nonprofits consider a grand plan for strengthening their capacity, they should ask whether they have the basics in place and how they will know the effort is successful, if it is. Organizational improvement always creates stress, but it need not always create surprise. Practice may not make perfect, but it may teach organizations how to pull the levers.

As the next chapter suggests, nonprofits cannot always improve the odds of success by themselves, especially if they are younger, smaller, or in financial distress. Moreover, whatever their age, size, and financial condition, nonprofits can hardly reap the benefits of outside contact if the outside world has little to offer by way of useful advice; neither can an organizational investment yield durable improvement if the sector as a whole does not solve the collective good problem associated with the coming labor shortage. Hard as they try to make their individual efforts succeed, nonprofits rise and fall in part with the sector as a whole, as do the odds of capacity-building success.

5 | Improving the Odds of Success

Despite its potential impact on organizational effectiveness, capacity building is far from automatic or easy. Roughly a quarter of the 318 efforts chronicled in this book were either somewhat successful or less, two-fifths of the survey respondents said their organization's effort taught them that change is very stressful for their staff, and more than half said they learned that change is more difficult to achieve than expected.

Some of these complaints are embedded in the basic rules of the sector, rules that Clara Miller of the Nonprofit Finance Fund says create a shadow universe of unintended consequences in which surpluses are not surpluses at all, but liabilities against future funding, and in which infrastructure is a sign of weakness, not strength. Consider the rules governing investment in infrastructure. As Miller argues, "The nonprofit rules of business largely prohibit investment needed to increase efficiency as growth occurs; third parties paying for a service prohibit or put limits on spending for anything but 'direct program,' not realizing that there are costs of growing in this highly regulated business."[1] Some donors simply pretend that administrative costs do not exist, while others imagine that capacity is somehow created by magic: I grow, therefore I think.

123

These kinds of restrictions will not melt away with hope, of course. They require collective action and advocacy across the sector. Just as businesses must spend money to make money, nonprofits must build capacity to have capacity. "If you look around, you can see how we've changed," said the head of a Baltimore arts organization when asked how capacity building affected her organization. "Our budget has doubled. Our staff has doubled. Our square feet have doubled. Our programs in the community have, God knows, quadrupled. Now I don't know if it is going to stay that way. We are getting ready to put up another building, and it has been hard to raise the money to do that. You can see that we don't have a big organizational surplus. Plus I have this gifted, wonderful, marvelous board chair who tells me he is done in 2005."

As this short chapter suggests, there are ways to improve the odds that organizations like this will not only survive but thrive. Doing so requires action at several levels: inside individual nonprofits, across the sector's capacity-building infrastructure, and among the collected parties who care about the sector as a whole.

Strategies for Success

Every research project has its limitations, not the least of which is the initial choice of methodology. This assessment is no different. In an ideal world, once again, the survey sample would have been much bigger, the research would have begun well before each organization started its improvement effort, and the analysis would have included objective and subjective measures of impact, not to mention site visits to validate the findings.

The question is not whether the research underpinning this report could have been more robust, but whether the evidence is sufficient to make the case for capacity building. I believe the answer is yes. The evidence clearly suggests that capacity building increases organizational capacity, which in turn influences organizational effectiveness, which in turn influences program performance, which in turn may have some impact on public confidence. Even if confidence does not rise with success, it most certainly declines with failure.

Much of this evidence is based on perceptions, which can and do reflect self-interest. But even given the appropriate caveats about self-reporting, the evidence is too strong to discount. Except for the allure of leadership as the great cure-all for what ails nonprofits, the relationships between capacity building and organizational capacity are almost exactly where one would expect them to be, given the prevailing wisdom about how strategic planning, media relations, reorganization, new programs, and so forth affect organizational outputs.

In turn, the relationships between these organizational outputs and the two broad measures of organizational effectiveness (organizational management and program impacts) are almost exactly where one would expect. And the relationships between these organizational outcomes and overall performance are strong.

Assuming that the chain holds, the question is what might be done to increase the odds that organizations will succeed. This book suggests three broad answers, the first dealing with improving the odds of success for particularly vulnerable organizations, the second with strengthening the nonprofit infrastructure in which capacity building takes place, and the third with recruiting talented employees as the baby boomers begin to retire.

Helping Vulnerable Nonprofits

Regardless of their age, size, or budgetary conditions, capacity building is more likely to succeed when it involves objective evidence, more contact with the outside world, outside funding, adequate resources regardless of the source, and advance planning. But all five are particularly important for vulnerable organizations, meaning organizations that are younger, smaller, or under budgetary stress.

First, consider the role of hard evidence on success, which is information essential to selecting and monitoring organizational improvement. Recall that the odds of success were greater for efforts rated by respondents who drew on hard evidence (formal evaluation or objective evidence), compared with those who used softer evidence (their own assessment).

Although hard evidence improved the odds of success among all 318 efforts covered in this book, it held particular promise for vulnerable organizations. Among organizations fifteen years old or younger, for example, 28 percent of efforts rated with hard evidence were judged to be completely successful, compared with 18 percent of efforts rated with softer evidence. Among organizations with fewer than 100 employees, 27 percent of efforts rated with hard evidence were judged to be completely successful, compared with just 7 percent of efforts rated with softer evidence. And among organizations with stable or declining budgets, 73 percent of efforts rated with hard evidence were judged to be mostly or completely successful, compared with 54 percent of those rated with softer evidence.

Second, think about contact with the outside world, which also alters the odds of success. Although some forms of contact are impossible without funding and others depend on a vibrant regional infrastructure worth contacting, contact increases the odds of success in younger organizations and older ones. The more organizations reach out, the more they learn; the more they learn, the greater the odds that they will succeed in their capacity building. Among organizations fifteen years old or younger, 66 percent of efforts that involved one or no outside contacts were rated as mostly or completely successful, compared with 90 percent of efforts that involved six or seven contacts. Among organizations with fewer than 100 employees, 66 percent of efforts that involved two or fewer outside resources were rated as mostly or completely successful, compared with 83 percent of efforts that involved six or seven contacts. And among organizations with stable or declining budgets, 46 percent of the efforts that involved one or no outside contacts were rated as mostly or completely successful, compared with 86 percent of those with six or seven contacts.

Third, consider the role of outside funding, which is much more important to capacity building than one might imagine given the relatively low cost of the 318 efforts. Not only does outside funding often provide the marginal dollars needed to move upward from somewhat adequate to very adequate financial support, it also stimulates contact with the outside world. In doing so, it forces organizations to do a bit of advance planning, develop logic chains and potential measures, focus their energies, and actually make a pitch. To paraphrase Alfred Lord Tennyson, 'tis better to have applied and lost than never to have applied at all.

So it is always better to get the money. Although the relationship between the mere presence of outside funding and success exists for organizations of all ages and sizes, it is particularly pronounced for young nonprofits. Among organizations fifteen years old or younger, 26 percent of efforts that received any outside funding at all were rated as completely successful, compared with 17 percent of those with no outside funding. Among organizations with fewer than 100 employees, 77 percent of efforts that received any outside funding at all were rated mostly or completely successful, compared with just 22 percent of those with no outside funding. And among organizations with stable or declining budgets, 58 percent of the efforts with any outside funding at all were rated as mostly or completely successful, compared with 40 percent of those with no outside funding.

For younger, smaller, more fragile organizations, a bit of outside funding can spell the difference between a successful climb back upward or continued stagnation or decline. It is always the marginal dollar that matters most—it is the dollar that might provide an hour or two for outside contact, the chance to think through the measurement question, a quick consultation with a consultant, a board retreat, or even a trip to the bookstore or Amazon.com.

Fourth, consider financial resources regardless of the source. No matter what the size, age, or budgetary condition of the organization, adequate funding improves the odds of success. Among organizations fifteen years old or younger, just 10 percent of the efforts with somewhat adequate funding or less were rated as completely successful, compared with 54 percent of the efforts with very adequate funding. Among organizations with fewer than 100 employees, just 8 percent of the efforts with somewhat adequate funding or less were rated as completely successful, compared with 29 percent of the efforts with very adequate funding. Unfortunately, only seven of the seventy-seven organizations with stable or declining budgets had very adequate funding for their efforts, rendering statistical comparisons impossible.

Finally, consider the impact of advance planning. Even a small amount of planning can go a long way to improving the odds of success. Among organizations fifteen years old or younger, 57 percent of the efforts with little or nearly no planning were rated as mostly or completely successful, compared with 81 percent of the efforts that involved a fair amount or a great deal of planning. Among organizations with fewer than 100 employees, 71 percent of the efforts with little or no planning were rated as mostly or completely successful, compared with 78 percent of those that involved a fair amount or a great deal of planning. And among organizations with stable or declining budgets, 54 percent of the efforts that involved little or nearly no planning were rated as mostly or completely successful, compared with 88 percent of the efforts that involved a fair amount or a great deal of planning.

Strengthening the Nonprofit Infrastructure

Increasing the odds of success involves more than internal organizational strategy. It also depends on the nonprofit sector's regional and national infrastructure, which consists of the financial, intellectual, educational, and technical supports needed for successful capacity building. Outside contact depends on the intellectual energy to make it worthwhile, the educational institutions to disseminate and inform it, and the technical support to apply it. While outside funding depends on donors, governments, and philanthropists who are ready and able to provide the dollars, and although organizations are free to measure to their heart's content, the national and regional infrastructure can provide needed standardization to ensure that the results make a difference in addressing the crisis of confidence described at the very beginning of this book.

Donors might be willing to put more funding into infrastructure if the infrastructure itself were strong enough to make its own case. Unfortunately, even the private sector has trouble making the case for its national and regional capacity-building infrastructure.

The best, and almost the only, research making the case comes from the total quality movement. According to Robert Cole, "Many factors operated to delay recognition of quality as a competitive factor," he writes of the early years of the quality movement, "and worked against learning effective responses to this challenge. . . . Not only were managers hamstrung by incomplete information, but they were also prisoners of existing values, norms, and practices that strongly conditioned their search to understand the quality problem and its solutions."[2]

The U.S. quality movement began to take hold through what Cole calls an innovation and diffusion community: "They created standards, identified bottlenecks, introduced new methodologies, publicized success stories, focused efforts, evolved forums for networking, and provided overall infrastructural support to users." Even then, as Cole notes, as "expertise about how to do quality improvement diffused among firms, we witnessed ironically the death of the quality movement. By the mid- and late-1990s, quality disappeared as a major topic in the media and was less and less a focus of top management's attention."

However, the national infrastructure does more than simply promote specific improvements. It also helps to create a positive climate for the sector as a whole, which in turn generates resources for change. As such, the national infrastructure contributes to organizational improvement at two levels: (1) it supplies much of the political, intellectual, human, and financial capital needed to implement successful change, and (2) it strengthens the environment in which nonprofits operate, which creates a greater stock of financial, intellectual, educational, and technical capital on which to draw.

In theory, for example, a stronger nonprofit infrastructure could lower the costs of learning by improving the quality of advice through publications, train-the-trainer efforts, and better materials, while providing greater access to the most helpful sources of advice (for example, management support centers are well rated, but infrequently used). The infrastructure could also create common learning space where nonprofits can draw on best practices more efficiently. By lowering the cost of learning, the infrastructure could raise the odds that individual capacity-building efforts will succeed, thereby lowering the aggregate cost of building capacity throughout the sector.

A stronger infrastructure might also address the collective good problems that are only now becoming clear as the nonprofit sector faces the long-awaited retirement of the huge baby boom generation. The resulting work force shortages threaten every corner of the nonprofit sector, yet few individual nonprofits have the resources to fight the talent war with government and the private sector on their own. Few can help debt-burdened recruits pay down their college loans, and fewer still have the funding to provide the signing and relocation bonuses now routinely paid by both government and business. Unless the nonprofit infrastructure figures out how to solve the recruiting problem through collective action, the sector is sure to face a human capital crisis of extraordinary proportions.

Finally, a stronger nonprofit infrastructure could create the incentives and measurements needed for successful capacity building, whether by setting standards, establishing rigorous awards programs, promoting best practices, or calling out problems that undermine effectiveness. Doing so clearly requires a stronger base of research. It is no surprise, for example, that it is nearly impossible to calculate rates of return on capacity-building investments. Unlike the private sector, which produces mountains of data on itself, not to mention the statistics it gets from government agencies such as the Bureau of Labor Statistics and Bureau of Economic Analysis, the nonprofit sector knows little about its own work force and even less about its impact on the national, state, and local economies. According to a recent analysis by Paul DiMaggio, Janet Weiss, and Charles Clotfelter, "Nonprofit scholars have much data with which to produce research, albeit not the data of their dreams. The nonprofit sector is continually changing in ways that definitions embedded in data-collection systems do not reflect." Yet, as they also argue, "The data resources are richer than most scholars recognize. There is more scope for making comparisons across subsectors than researchers have thus far exploited. And there are unrealized opportunities for exploring the division of labor across sectors and across different kinds of institutions."[3] Collecting better data and conducting innovative research both require investment, however, as well as advocacy on behalf of philanthropic investment in ongoing analysis.

Doing so also involves continued progress in defining basic standards and definitions of ordinary best practice. The nonprofit sector does not need to wait for the U.S. Congress to define administrative costs, for example. Neither does it need its own version of the American Competitiveness and Corporate Accountability Act of 2002, better known as Sarbanes-Oxley, which imposed sweeping reforms on publicly traded corporations to restore public confidence in the wake of the Enron and WorldCom accounting scandals. But it most certainly does need to heighten its focus on the kind of standards that have been developed from within the sector by the Maryland Association of Nonprofit Organizations and the Minnesota Council of Nonprofits. In doing so, the national infrastructure could help to translate best practices from other sectors into a uniquely "nonprofit-like" approach that acknowledges the presence of a dual bottom line in individual organizations. Such an effort could also address the new Golden Rule for nonprofits: "Do unto yourself before Congress and state attorneys general do unto you."

Recruiting the Future Work Force

No amount of strategy or infrastructure will improve the odds of success for long unless the nonprofit sector gets better, and faster, at recruiting the next generation of employees. The sector is facing the same "brain drain" that is gripping government and business but has yet to mobilize itself for action. Even the federal government, which is hardly known as a leading indicator of personnel innovation, has launched a broad recruiting initiative featuring on-the-spot hiring, loan forgiveness, and signing bonuses.

Contrary to conventional wisdom, however, higher pay and loan forgiveness are not the keys to recruiting success. According to a May 2003 survey of 1,002 about-to-graduate college students, 67 percent of seniors ranked the opportunity to help people as the most important consideration in finding a job. Job benefits, such as health insurance and vacation time, the opportunity to obtain challenging work, and the opportunity to learn new skills tied for second (63 percent each), followed by job security (60 percent), the opportunity for advancement (56 percent), and the opportunity to repay college loans (43 percent). Salary was ranked last, at just 30 percent.[4]

Students with high levels of debt were no more interested in salary than students without any debt at all. Rather, they were interested in jobs that provided the opportunity to repay college loans: 67 percent of students with more than $20,000 in debt said repaying college loans was a very important consideration in their decision about where to work after graduation, compared with just 11 percent who had no debt at all.

Although debt was clearly a consideration, it was far from the only concern. Even for students with high levels of debt, the opportunity to help people was still the top factor in considering a job in any sector. These respondents did not just say, "Show me the cause"; they also said, "Show me the impact."

The good news is that nonprofit work shows very well: 75 percent of nonprofit employees strongly disagreed that their work was boring, compared with 57 and 58 percent of federal government and business employees, respectively; 74 percent of nonprofit employees reported that morale was very or somewhat high among their coworkers, compared with 72 percent of business employees and 60 percent of federal government employees; 73 percent said their organization encouraged employees to take risks or try new ways of doing their work a great deal or a fair amount of the time, compared with 58 and 62 percent of federal government and business employees; 68 percent of nonprofit employees strongly agreed that they were given the chance to do the things that they do best, compared with 46 and 52 percent of federal government and business employees; and 58 percent of nonprofit employees strongly disagreed that their job was a dead end with no future, compared with 47 and 54 percent of federal government and business employees.

This enthusiasm for nonprofit work was echoed elsewhere in the May 2003 survey. The 1,002 college seniors were clearly interested in the kind of work that nonprofits do. The nonprofit sector was seen as the best place to go for someone who wanted a chance to help people, make a difference, and gain the respect of family and friends, government was seen as the most attractive place for someone who wanted good benefits and the chance to serve the country, and private contractors were seen as best for someone who wanted the best salary.

In addition, the nonprofit sector was seen as the best of the three sectors at spending money wisely, helping people, and being fair in its decisions: 60 percent said the nonprofit sector was the best at spending money wisely, compared with just 6 percent who said government; 61 percent said the nonprofit sector was the best at being fair in its decisions, compared with just 22 percent who said government; and 76 percent said the nonprofit sector was the best at helping people, compared with just 16 percent who said government. Contractors were viewed as the worst at being fair in their decisions (10 percent) and helping people (4 percent) but ranked above government on spending money wisely (29 percent).

It is one thing to offer the kind of jobs that talented people want and quite another to build a hiring process that works. Although nonprofit employees saw their organization's hiring process as simple, fast, and very fair, there are warning signs. Younger employees in the sample were less likely than older respondents to say their organization was doing a good job at retaining employees, for example, and were more likely to say that it would be easy for them to get another job in a different organization.

The college seniors also saw problems. Just 44 percent of the seniors said they knew a great deal or a fair amount about finding a job with a nonprofit, only 2 percent said that the nonprofit sector was the best of the three sectors for salaries, and just 5 percent said it was the best for benefits. Even more troubling for the nonprofit sector, only 22 percent of the seniors said nonprofits were the place to go for serving the country. Just as government has lost its meaning as a destination for helping people, the nonprofit sector has little identity as a place for serving the country.

Capacity Building as a Collective Good

Building stronger nonprofits is a nearly classic collective good problem. Simply put, everyone wants stronger nonprofits, but almost no one wants to pay for them. The public thinks nonprofits are not wasteful but want the money to go straight to the cause; many donors restrict their dollars for program expenses only and want somebody else to pick up the heat, light, and rent; boards and executives are sometimes reluctant to divert scarce resources to what they see as luxuries; clients are often willing to tolerate some level of inefficiency to keep programs going; and the work force itself has come to expect second-class support in return for the chance to accomplish something worthwhile.

The nonprofit sector would do well to look across the Atlantic Ocean at a very different model. In 2004 the British government launched two new funding programs to strengthen its voluntary and community sector.

The first involved direct funding for the purchase of new equipment and facilities, while the second focused on strengthening national organizations that promote capacity building. As Parliamentary Undersecretary Fiona Mactaggert explains the prime minister's rationale for a nearly $300 million initiative, government has an obligation to strengthen the nonprofit sector: "If the voluntary and community sector is to thrive and play its role in achieving a shared vision of reform and renewal, it needs high-quality and sustainable support services. . . . It is in the interests of us all, working in partnership with the sector and its infrastructure, to build and sustain the capacity of strong, independent, and dynamic voluntary and community organisations and enterprises."[5]

The initiative not only demonstrates the government's commitment to a vibrant sector but also recognizes its dependency on nonprofits for its own performance. Nonprofits are often the face of government in the United Kingdom. They are often the first point of contact in community health, children's services, disaster relief, HIV-AIDS, affordable housing, economic development, and job training, and they are intimately involved in a host of other government priorities. To the extent that nonprofits fail to deliver efficient and effective services, the British government fails too.

The U.S. federal government is unlikely to launch a similar program without support on both sides of the political aisle. Unfortunately, most political leaders know little about the sector, and what they do know is fueled by the latest scandal. Much as they celebrate volunteerism, they have almost nothing to say about the organizations in which volunteerism takes place. Much as they celebrate smaller government, they have almost nothing to say about the organizations that fill government's place. Much as they talk about preparing for terrorist attacks, they have almost nothing to say about nonprofits as first responders. They may say it takes a village to create a more hopeful future, but they almost never mention the nonprofit that the village almost certainly contains.

This general ignorance confirms the sector's need to strengthen its own national infrastructure. The British government is investing in national infrastructure organizations not because it wants to create greater lobbying pressure or pork-barrel spending, but because it knows that national infrastructure organizations are a key force for improving performance among local organizations. And one of the reasons it is investing in the infrastructure of its local organizations is that it realizes just how much its future depends on high-performing nonprofits. If the

British government gets it, perhaps it is time for the U.S. government to get it too.

With or without federal funding, nonprofits will almost certainly continue to build capacity the way they have always done it: by cobbling together the resources the best they can. The good news is that the nonprofit sector has an extraordinary hunger to improve—witness the extraordinary range of activity that led up to the 318 initiatives discussed earlier. The bad news is that far too much of that work involves little more than a wing and a prayer. For too many nonprofits, capacity building is still a hobby done with little planning, outside contact, or funding. That is no way to build the kind of momentum needed to reverse public cynicism about the sector's fealty or to ensure that nonprofits reap the rewards of their work.

Boards can play a particularly significant role in addressing these collective good issues as they work their connections to the outside world. Although executive directors do discuss certain types of capacity building with their board, they appear to view organizational improvement as an executive function best left to the senior staff. At the same time, there is little evidence that nonprofits use their board members to create networks of support for capacity building more generally, to encourage outside funding, or to create collective goods. My hunch is that boards could do much more both inside and outside on behalf of the sector, in part by requiring due diligence as executive directors make capacity-building investments, in part by pressuring their peers to invest in organizational improvement, and in part by becoming more aggressive advocates on behalf of the sector as a whole.

Conclusions

Ultimately, the best way to improve the odds of capacity-building success is to pick the right answer for the right problem at the right time and for the right reason. Many change efforts almost certainly fail because an organization turned to strategic planning when it should have reorganized, changed leaders when it should have changed technologies, created new programs when it should have eliminated old products, launched a new brand when it should have fixed its accounting system.

Picking the right answer involves a two-step, highly interactive process. First, an organization must know what kind of problem or opportunity it actually faces, which requires at least some assessment of organizational time and place. Whereas start-ups may need more structure, established organizations may need less; whereas start-ups may need simpler communication strategies, established organizations may need complex strategies.

Second, an organization must know which intervention might actually fit the problem or opportunity it has, which again requires an assessment of time and place. Whereas start-ups might do best with relatively inexpensive forms of strategic planning, such as assumption-based planning, established organizations may need something much stronger, such as exploratory analysis or robust adaptive planning; whereas start-ups may need help with board and leadership recruitment, established organizations may need succession planning.

As the next chapter suggests, this kind of interactive matching requires a different image of the organizational life cycle. Instead of viewing organizations as biological organisms that move steadily toward a confrontation with their own mortality, the next chapter argues that organizations move up and down a developmental spiral as they address the problems and opportunities associated with growth and decline.

Although movement is related to age and size, it is also tied to successful or unsuccessful capacity building. To the extent that organizations invest in building capacity, I believe that they can age and move up the spiral, survive a crisis or shock, and ensure against decline. To the extent that they ignore organizational capacity or wait until the last minute to act, they can just as easily move down the spiral.

6 The Spiral of Sustainable Excellence

Imagine nonprofit life as a journey up and down a spiral. All organizations would start with a simple idea for some new program or service and then move up the spiral toward greater and greater impact. Also imagine five landings, or stops, along the climb: the organic phase of life in which they struggle to create a presence in their environment, the enterprising phase in which they seek to expand their size and scope, the intentional phase in which they try to focus themselves on what they do best, the robust phase in which they strengthen their organizational infrastructure to hedge against the unexpected, and the reflective phase in which they address longer-term issues of succession and legacy.

Viewed as a spiral, nonprofit development would be anything but a fixed march ever upward. Many nonprofits would linger at one stage or another for long periods of time. Some organizations would make it up the first flight and remain at the organic landing for what might seem like an eternity. Others might quickly move to the enterprising stage, becoming the "hot" organization in their community or field, and stay there for a lifetime or at least for an executive director or two. Others would make the difficult climb from the enterprising stage to intentionality by focusing their attention on the programs they care about most, while jettisoning and spinning off others. Still others would enhance their capacity to withstand crises and shocks, handle risks, recruit and retain the most talented employees for the long term, and shape the future through their advocacy. And relatively few would reach the reflective stage by expanding their mission to include broad questions of long-term legacy.

Viewed as a spiral, nonprofit development would also vary in both direction and speed. Some nonprofits would rise quickly through the stages, perhaps because of a large grant or unexpected gift; others would move slowly, if at all, from one stage to the other. More important, some nonprofits would move down the spiral from time to time, perhaps because of a crisis or shock, a leader's departure, a change in government or donor priorities, or an investigation. Some would even jump down the spiral to their organic roots from time to time to ask themselves again why they exist, whom they serve, and how they intend to make a difference in the world. Indeed, I believe an important part of being a reflective nonprofit is being acutely aware of the organic history of the organization.

This image of a development spiral did not spring full-blown from my imagination. It emerged from site visits to twenty-five high-performing nonprofits selected from the 250 organizations identified in my *Pathways to Nonprofit Excellence* project. The site visits covered nine cities— Atlanta, Chicago, Indianapolis, Los Angeles, Minneapolis, New York, San Diego, San Francisco, and Washington. The site visits began with a trip to Chicago on September 14, 2001, and concluded in March 2003 in Atlanta.

The twenty-five nonprofits were hand-picked to provide a wide range of experience and included well-known national organizations such as Care, Doctors without Borders, Environmental Defense, the Girl Scouts, the Nature Conservancy, OMB Watch, and Share Our Strength; regional exemplars such as the New York's Big Apple Circus, Chicago's Friends of the Chicago River, Heartland Alliance, Lakefront Supportive Housing, and Vital Bridges (which was named Open Hand Chicago at the time of the site visit), the Indianapolis Children's Museum and Second Helpings, the Los Angeles Alliance for a New Economy, Pillsbury Neighborhood Services in Minneapolis, and the San Diego Opera; and well-known local organizations such as the Bay Area's Pacific Repertory Theater, Asian-Pacific-Islander Wellness Center, and Pact Adoption Alliance, Los Angeles's Community Coalition and Tree Musketeers,

Chicago's Ancona School and Instituto del Progreso Latino, and Washington's Calvary Women's Services.

As the list suggests, the twenty-five included large organizations and small, young organizations and old, and a wide variety of missions—from HIV-AIDS education to international relief—but it is easy to argue that all were achieving significant program impacts. However, at least eight of the twenty-five were achieving those impacts in spite of significant organizational frustrations, and none was perfect in every way. According to my observations following half- to full-day visits with each organization, seven of the twenty-five high performers did not appear to have a current strategic plan and two more paid little attention to the plan they had; ten had yet to develop a diversified funding base; ten were struggling to clarify board and staff responsibilities (no doubt in part because nine did not do any board training); thirteen had accounting weaknesses of some kind; fourteen did not have clear job descriptions in the files; fourteen did not provide disability insurance to their employees; fourteen held five or fewer board meetings a year; and seventeen did not have a system for measuring outcomes.[1]

Once again, the question is not whether nonprofits can achieve program results in spite of organizational weaknesses, budgetary shocks, staff turnover, or even terrorist attacks. Rather, the question is what would help them to move up the developmental spiral toward sustainable high performance. For some, the climb may involve relatively small investments in a new accounting package, board and staff training, a bit of strategic thinking, or more internal communication; for others, it may involve a merger, reorganization, a spin-off, a new program, a change in mission, a new executive, or a painful decision to suspend operations.

As this chapter argues, however, some forms of capacity building are much more important for moving from the organic to the enterprising stage or for stopping the fall backward, while others are much more appropriate for the climb from intentional to robust. As such, successful capacity building depends in large part on picking the right improvement effort at the right time.

Images of Development

Like most organizations today, nonprofits face an uncertain future. No one knows what might happen to the economy as the federal budget deficit rises, how far Congress might go in tightening accounting and expenditure rules, whether young Americans will ever get the giving habit, how nonprofits will handle the baby boom retirements, and how many more nonprofits the sector can absorb with a shrinking labor force. And that is just a sampling of the known unknowns.

No matter what happens to the sector as a whole, individual non-profits can never be quite sure what the future holds. This was certainly the case for the twenty-five high-performing nonprofits. The Nature Conservancy was about to enter a period of remarkable turbulence fol-lowing a *Washington Post* investigation of its management and operat-ing practices; the San Diego Opera was little more than eighteen months away from a $10 million bequest from McDonald's heiress Joan B. Kroc; the Pacific Repertory Theater in Carmel, California, had mailed its annual fund-raising appeal only days before the September 11 attacks and was behind $65,000 by the time I arrived in November; Care was about to launch a new branding campaign to change its focus from deliv-ering food to ending global poverty; and Open Hand Chicago was about to merge with two other AIDS nutrition programs to keep up with an ever-changing epidemic.[2]

Some of the events were completely unexpected. The Pacific Reper-tory Theater could not have known about September 11, and the Nature Conservancy did not know of the *Washington Post* investigation until days before the story broke. But most of the events involved at least some advance warning. Open Hand Chicago had been talking about a merger for some time, while Care had been working on its new mission since 1996. As a senior Care executive remembered, "I think we would still exist if we hadn't changed, but we would have fossilized and, I think, would have become increasingly less relevant. The opposite has hap-pened. We've become, if anything, more relevant. The post–September 11 period has only underlined how really important these changes have been. Our vision is a world of hope, tolerance, and social justice where poverty has been overcome and all people live in dignity and security."

Moreover, all twenty-five organizations clearly understood that change happens. As a senior executive at Chicago's Lakefront Support-ive Housing remarked on September 19, 2001, "Last week changed the whole world. Our long-term plan is suddenly up for grabs. People say that organizations should get used to change, but sometimes change is just horrible. Good hitting is about good form, and good pitching is about disrupting form. Sometimes I feel like change is always about dis-rupting form. I come in every day and feel like I'm doing battle with change. We just keep growing, and I have to keep figuring out each step of the way."

If change is inevitable, the question is what nonprofits can do to improve the odds that they will survive the inevitable surprises, exploit the upturns, and shape the environment to their favor. Organizations do not have to be old and large to hedge against surprises and exploit good fortune. Indeed, being old and large can produce a notable sluggishness in doing both. But they do need to know where they are in organizational time and place to pick the right course. If they do not know where they are, they cannot know how far they must go and what they must do to get there.

Sorting Destinations

Nonprofits cannot be blamed for all that goes wrong as they move up or down the spiral, nor can they be given absolute credit for all that goes right. As figure 6-1 suggests, nonprofits move up and down a developmental spiral in part by asking the right questions, addressing potential threats, and choosing the right strategies for building organizational capacity.

Whatever their ultimate goal—be it to end poverty, feed the hungry, change public policy, or produce great art—every organization starts with the same simple goal: to exist. I believe the most important questions are asked at this very first landing: How will we make a difference? Who does what in the organization? Why do we exist? How will we know we are successful, if we are? The answers do not have to be perfect or even complete. But they must be asked if the organization wants to create early momentum toward impact and asked frequently if the organization is to claim any purpose but survival.

Organic nonprofits face inevitable trade-offs between passion and caution. If start-ups had to wait until their programs and systems were perfect, they would never launch at all. Yet if they launch without asking hard questions about their ability to deliver on the promises they make, they almost certainly will disappoint or disappear. They must be visible enough to attract support, while creating the capacity to produce results.

Unfortunately, many organic nonprofits launch without testing the load-bearing assumptions that support their basic program goals—for example, whether the world will behave as they hope. Too many also launch without making the basic decisions about tracking impacts and

FIGURE 6-1. The Developmental Spiral

FIFTH LANDING:
The Reflective Nonprofit

GOAL
Legacy

QUESTIONS
Environment: How can we lead?
Structure: How do we get younger?
Leadership: How do we change the future?
Systems: How do we manage freedom?

THREATS
Environment: Imperialism
Structure: Complacency and routine
Leadership: Self-aggrandizement
Systems: Self-preservation

CAPACITY BUILDING
Environment: Exploring
Structure: Sorting
Leadership: Advocating and elevating
Systems: Testing and renewing

FOURTH LANDING:
The Robust Nonprofit

GOAL
Endurance

QUESTIONS
Environment: What are our futures?
Structure: How do we stay agile?
Leadership: What are our values?
Systems: How do we insure against vulnerabilities?

THREATS
Environment: Isolation
Structure: Overconfidence
Leadership: Self-satisfaction
Systems: Aging and under-investment

CAPACITY BUILDING
Environment: Insuring
Structure: Learning and team building
Leadership: Challenging and inspiring
Systems: Insuring and monitoring

THIRD LANDING:
The Intentional Nonprofit

GOAL
Focus

QUESTIONS
Environment: How do we fit?
Structure: Can we increase our impact by concentrating?
Leadership: How do we remain faithful?
Systems: How have we done thus far?

THREATS
Environment: Backlash
Structure: Specialization
Leadership: Conflict and resistance
Systems: Underdevelopment

CAPACITY BUILDING
Environment: Focusing
Structure: Reorganizing
Leadership: Clarifying and explaining
Systems: Tightening and investing

SECOND LANDING:
The Enterprising Nonprofit

GOAL
Impact

QUESTIONS
Environment: Where will we expand?
Structure: How much can we do?
Leadership: How do we remain authentic?
Systems: How will we cope with breadth?

THREATS
Environment: Diffusion
Structure: Burnout
Leadership: Overpromising
Systems: Underinvestment

CAPACITY BUILDING
Environment: Mapping
Structure: Innovating
Leadership: Risk taking and persuading
Systems: Measuring

FIRST LANDING:
The Organic Nonprofit

GOAL
Presence

QUESTIONS
Environment: How will we make a difference?
Structure: Who does what?
Leadership: Why do we exist?
Systems: How will we know we are successful, if we are?

THREATS
Environment: Invisibility
Structure: Confusion
Leadership: Overconfidence
Systems: Shallowness

CAPACITY BUILDING
Environment: Questioning
Structure: Deploying
Leadership: Defining
Systems: Requiring

accounting for time and money. And too many launch without creating basic expectations governing the organization. Although their leaders must work hard to build identity, these young nonprofits must outline the organizational infrastructure that will hold them together as they confront a turbulent, competitive environment. This means investing in simple reporting routines, clarifying board and staff responsibilities, and building basic operating systems, all of which respond to simple capacity-building interventions.

Assuming that they garner enough support to grow, many organic nonprofits advance to the enterprising landing where they promptly get stuck. Having achieved enough credibility to compete for resources, enterprising nonprofits face a number of challenges as they seek to expand their impact. Some find it nearly impossible to say no to the funding they need to survive, while others branch out into fields well beyond their original program intent, and still others become the hot nonprofit that donors just have to fund. But what goes up in the enterprising stage often comes crashing down as the next hot nonprofit shows up.

There is nothing wrong with stretching the organization into what I call the "zone just beyond possible," particularly if the organization is making a measurable difference through its work. But the stretching can create confusion, underinvestment in core administrative systems, and employee burnout as the organization tries to meet all the deadlines it has accepted. Having started out with a clear sense of direction, enterprising nonprofits often evolve into multiservice agencies that have drifted far from the core mission they once embraced.

Growth is not harmful if it takes a nonprofit where it wants to go, however, and nonprofits have a better chance of getting where they want to go if they have a careful map of their environment, if innovation fits with their program goals, and if their leaders work to reconcile new initiatives with the old. They are also much more likely to expand gracefully if they have the measurement and tracking systems to know where they are at any given point in time and what they did to get there. This means investing in more elegant analysis of environmental threats and opportunities, internal organization, board and staff development, and measurement, all of which respond to capacity building.

The reason so many nonprofits get stuck at the enterprising stage is that they cannot find the focus needed for intentional action. Becoming intentional often involves a confrontation with the dependencies created during the enterprising phase, particularly for organizations that grew by stretching well beyond their original program goals. Often nonprofits can only become more intentional by releasing staff, board members, programs, and leaders, thereby creating the organizational capacity to invest in the activities they care about most.

Letting go requires a mix of courage, commitment, and measurement. Intentional nonprofits can face intense board and employee resistance, as well as a community backlash. They may find it difficult to reassign employees who were hired for their specialized skills, nearly impossible to combine units with very different program histories, and intensely stressful to spend scarce resources on organizational infrastructure. Intentional nonprofits often discover that each of their enterprises has its own language and culture and almost always conclude that streamlining, reorganizing, downsizing, and focusing are easier said than done.

Although organizations often argue that these choices are easier when done under budget pressure, they are tough choices nonetheless. Hence tools that permit thoughtful sorting of priorities and analysis of organizational capacity help leaders to address conflict and anxiety and to tighten administrative systems, all of which involve various forms of capacity building.

The move from enterprise to intention does not have to be done alone. It is often done through mergers and strategic alliances with other organizations that are also spread too thinly or through expansion in a particular line of work. It is also often done with the support of a community foundation or venture philanthropy that is ready to commit resources to a more focused future. Such investments are rarely made without the underlying evidence to show program impacts and organizational productivity, however. To the extent that organic nonprofits set high expectations for evidence of impact and that enterprising nonprofits further the effort by adopting more sophisticated systems, they both raise the odds that they will attract the energy, if not the funding, for the next move upward.

Once at the intentional stage, nonprofits often begin to take steps toward robustness. As I define the term in *The Robust Organization*, robustness involves "the ability to withstand, even exploit, uncertainty."[3] Nonprofits exist in a world of many futures: some favorable, some threatening. Robust nonprofits prepare for uncertainty by hedging against vulnerabilities and shaping the environment for maximum effect.

Hedging against uncertainty involves more than fretting about surprises. It requires a basic willingness to think in futures (plural) tense, which, in turn, requires an agile organizational structure, concentration, and insurance against surprises. It also requires a greater focus on the longer term. Robust organizations must be able to run sprints, particularly when reacting to surprises, but their great strength is the marathon.

Unlike the elementary planning that helps organic nonprofits to test their program assumptions, for example, robust organizations prepare for multiple futures simultaneously. Most set aside at least some funds for the worst case, deepen their insurance against a range of catastrophes, and often create contingency plans for acting quickly to stem the financial damage from cost overruns and surprises such as rapid escalations in health care costs. They build financial systems that operate in real time, meaning that they can get accurate revenue statements at a moment's notice, and often create early warning systems, or signposts, that show trouble ahead. As they build, robust organizations also engage in basic risk analysis, weighing new program costs against potential benefits.

Robust organizations are perfectly capable of innovation, however. They often take enormous leaps of faith. But those leaps are well informed by careful analysis and measurement. Robust organizations are just as likely to believe in luck as their peers, but they often create the luck they need by building the organizational structure for maximum opportunism. Many also seek to shape their future by launching their first endowment campaign, buying their first building, deepening their board, or launching their first business venture.

Much as robustness helps organizations to cope with uncertainty, it can also breed isolation and hubris. The more robust the organization becomes, the less accountable it can become. It can lose its sense of direction, drift toward imperialism and self-righteousness, and abuse the opportunities that come with independence. Hence, even as they protect themselves against uncertainty and stay lean, robust organizations must continue to challenge and inspire themselves, while investing in basic accountability systems. The more they face into the environment through measurement, formal and informal contact with their markets, benchmarking against other organizations, and strategic thinking, the better.

As they push themselves to confront their own role in shaping the future, robust organizations eventually reach a more reflective position. Instead of seeing themselves as victims of uncertainty and surprise, reflective organizations focus on their own contributions to the future through advocacy, example, and legacy. Some even try to put themselves out of business by embracing audacious goals like eliminating global poverty or cooling the earth to normal temperature.

Having achieved the independence of robustness, reflective organizations often return to the organic questions that sparked their initial journey, challenging themselves to merge their present capabilities with their past intentions. They often do so by exploring the future through even more advanced planning techniques such as computer-assisted simulation, streamlining their administrative structures through organizational assessment and staff rotation, preparing for inevitable departures through succession planning, and renewing their management systems through upgrades and innovation.

Absent this self-discipline, reflective organizations can easily become imperial organizations, imposing their will on the rest of the field, while absorbing resources that might better go to other organizations. Not unlike large corporations, they may become so focused on self-preservation that they forget what brought them into being in the first place.

Nonprofits do not have to be large to be reflective, however. To the contrary, they may be quite small relative to the organizations against which they sometimes compete. They almost certainly act younger, whether by constantly streamlining, incubating new organizations within their own midst, fostering deliberate board and staff turnover, undertaking constant benchmarking against other organizations both inside and outside the field, entering new collaborations and strategic alliances, and contemplating mergers and spin-offs, all of which face the organization into the outside world. Reflective organizations remain reflective in part by revisiting the techniques that helped them to move upward through the organic, enterprising, intentional, and robust landings.

No matter how hard they try, nonprofits cannot prepare for every possible surprise or shock. They are often one economic crisis from a painful trip back down the spiral. Although endowments and insurance can make the trip a brief one, nonprofits can and do rise and fall on the developmental spiral with regularity. Indeed, one of the ways in which robust and reflective nonprofits prepare for misfortune is to plan for it. They do so by investing in renewal even during good times. They do not take success for granted or assume that their organization is working well just because they do not hear any complaints.

Reflections of Reality?

The notion that nonprofits move up and down a developmental spiral is a blend of several different images of organizations. Some readers will detect a life cycle embedded in words such as organic, robust, and reflective; others will sense organizational evolution at work in the environmental pressures that bear down on organizations at one landing or another; still others will think of engineering in the effort to build the scaffolding for improvement.[4]

The twenty-five organizations also used a range of images to describe their history. Perhaps because they were so young, the enterprising organizations in the sample tended to use aging as their favorite metaphor. "We see Pact as another one of our children," said one of the cofounders of the adoption advocacy agency located just north of San Francisco. "We've always recruited board members and staff who have been touched by the adoption experience. My point is simply that the organization has evolved as children evolve. Pact was a child ten years ago. We see ourselves as pre-adolescent now. As founders, we tend to be provisionary dominators, but it's really critical to us that Pact eventually be independent and able to stand on its own."

A senior executive at Second Helpings used almost the same language to describe the history of her Indianapolis food rescue and job training agency created in 1995. "We have gone from infancy to toddlers to feeling like eleven-year-olds. We are ready to be grown-ups but do not know how to react to it. The board started out as a working board, and that was necessary—we needed their bodies, we needed their hands, we needed their money, and we drained their heads. The board also had to grow up."

At the same time, Second Helpings felt it was not old enough for strategic planning. "We are still too young to have a strategic plan," the executive explained. "When your middle name is still 'Tweak,' how do you develop a strategic plan? We have to remain flexible. We have a mental idea of where we want to go but only look twenty-four months out." Would that most nonprofits could do as well without a plan: in July 2003 Second Helpings launched a $2.2 million capital campaign to buy and equip a new building; six months later, it moved in.

Friends of the Chicago River, an environmental advocacy group incorporated in 1988, faced a similar investment dilemma. Asked whether he thought start-ups should first work on management or program, a senior executive said, "It's a constant juggling act of nurture this here, nurture that there. Now we're nurturing program, now we're nurturing administration, and it's a constant juggling of the two. It takes a lot of skill to develop strong programs without having the management stuff in place. You have to operate a lot by intuition, which can put you in harm's way."

Growth eventually provided the resources for long-overdue investment. "In the beginning years, our bookkeeping and administration were
really a mess," this executive explained just before switching metaphors.
"We all agreed that if we had to slip on something, it was going to be on
certain types of paperwork. We waited until we could afford to take
those on, until our programs were stronger and people were saying
'Wow, you guys are doing a lot of great work.' Then we could say, 'Now
we have to fix up our infrastructure a little bit.'"

In contrast, the intentional organizations in the sample tended to use
geology or evolution as their historical metaphor. "Our first watershed
was putting up a tent at Lincoln Center," said a senior executive at the
Big Apple Circus, which gave its first performance twenty-five years ago
in Manhattan's Battery Park City. "It was recognition by an important
community—the arts community—that we belonged here. They would-
n't have allowed a commercial circus into that space. Suddenly we had a
flagship season, a Lincoln Center season. And we expanded from there."

As the schedule expanded, so did the organizational stress. "By the
sixth year," said the executive, "the board simply said 'You can't run a
business this way, at least not forever.' They supported what we did but
began to see that we weren't going to last at all if we continued to operate without help. We reached our second plateau when we hired an executive director. I can't remember who separated the functions of
managing the circus and managing the organization, but the watershed
event was the decision to go out and recruit a professional executive
director." In turn, the Big Apple increased its annual fund-raising targets,
bought a vacant factory to store its equipment and rehearse its shows,
and moved up to the intentional landing.

Billy Shore's Share Our Strength is on a similar intentional rise. Created in 1984 as an intermediary between donors and hundreds of other
organizations, Share Our Strength has raised more than $70 million over
the past two decades to fight hunger and poverty both in the United
States and abroad. Although much of the money has come from the
annual Taste of the Nation charity benefit, which involved 10,000 volunteers and sixty-five cities in 2004, Share Our Strength has been a pio-
neer in creating partnerships with private corporations such as American
Express and Tyson Foods.

Because it pushes 100 percent of its Taste of the Nation proceeds out
to grantees, Share Our Strength has never held much, if any, funding
in reserve. By the mid-1990s, it had no choice but to invest in its own

infrastructure. "I think it was more of the evolution of the organization in terms of its life," a senior executive said of the commitment. "We're not that old, especially when you look at the American Red Cross, Nature Conservancy, or any of these other national organizations that are fifty, 100 years old. For us, it was very much a kind of family-run business, a very small business, very fast paced, less attention to systems. Because we were sending so much money out, we were like an under-capitalized foundation. And we got to a point where we were of an age where we had to put some of these things in place."

Those systems included what one staffer called the "big ugly data-base" to keep track of income and outgo, a new retirement plan for employees, new information and fund-raising technology, and better planning. Like many intentional organizations, Share Our Strength had to divert resources from its core mission to administrative systems, which was anything but easy given its history. "We are really committed to turning money around quickly and doing grant making in the short term," said another senior executive. "And the number one priority has not been for us to have a reserve fund or an endowment. It's really been about pulling off this year's events and getting the money out the door. And that's the way it's been since we started." Asked about her own role in strengthening the organization, her answer was simple and straight-forward: "My goal is always to stabilize the organization, have money in place for the long-term needs of the organization, look at ways to insure that we're around for the long term, and perform the functions that we see as critical. That's why we're in business. Our goal is to try to stabilize our chances of being able to do that for the long term. So I do want to see a positive bottom line. I want to see us as being profitable."

Perhaps because they had already been around for the long term, the robust and reflective organizations in the sample tended to worry most about renewal and repair, using engineering as their preferred metaphor. Thus a senior executive at the Nature Conservancy focused on the need to become more disciplined in building administrative systems. "We did not have a human resource function here until recently; we had no direc-tor of human resources. That's in an organization of 3,000 people in twenty countries. We had forty-three websites, 20,000 budget accounts, no single e-mail system, no consistency in the technology on your desk. When something went down in the system, it took forever to find the problem, let alone fix it."

The decentralization had its benefits, not the least of which was sub-stantial robustness in an uncertain environment. "This organization is so large and so decentralized that it's got a low center of gravity. It's pretty hard to knock it over with a change in leadership or a crisis." But the robustness fell well short of reflection. As another senior executive explained, "The challenge is to stop doing things that we've always done that are not contributing toward the mission. The first step is to use 'zero-based planning' and take a fresh look at everything we're doing. We're not going to get rid of people, but we are going to change what people do. We would like to grow from 3,000 people to 10,000, but we want the 10,000 to be doing the right things and have everything aligned so they have the incentive to do the right things."

A senior executive at the San Diego Opera echoed the sentiment: "If you are going to really move an organization forward, you have to be on a constant learning curve. You have to be a perpetual student. If you don't want to do that, then you won't turn an institution around. You have to deal with so many conflicting personalities that unless you can show that you know your subject, unless you can give the references when you think they have to be stated, then you just become somebody who is buffeted from point to point."

To move forward, however, the San Diego Opera first had to move backward. It was doing eight operas a year when the new executive team arrived in the mid-1980s and immediately dropped down to four, which several executives described as "pruning the rose bush." It also adopted its first strategic plan, which it updates every three months. As one executive explained, "You have to have a long-range plan in the world of opera, especially for a company at this level. You have to book artists four years in advance. We're competing for the same artists as the New York Metropolitan Opera, San Francisco, Paris, Vienna, and we have to offer those contracts at least four years and sometimes five years in advance. So how do you do that if you don't have a plan, if you don't know how much money you will have coming in? That's when you get yourself in a big hole."

Open Hand Chicago faced a similar choice as the AIDS crisis changed. "We really had to contain costs," a senior executive described the budgetary crisis her organization faced after fifteen years in operation. "The organization just hadn't developed. It had grown, but it hadn't developed. When the organization started, it was on the north side of town because that was where the clients were. But the clients started moving, and it didn't." As this executive explained, the only way to move up was to move down. "We closed one office and moved up here. We just didn't spend money. We didn't hire staff. We cut $250,000 out of a $2 million budget. But that gave us a surplus, and we started to build everything that we needed to sustain the organization, most importantly to build a board that is engaged, vigilant, and productive."

The work also generated momentum toward a $4.2 million merger with two other AIDS organizations, which allowed Open Hand Chicago to reach 4,200 clients across the city and rebrand itself as Vital Bridges. As this executive recently reported, "While the first eighteen months have certainly been difficult, as expected, due to the economic environment and the sheer challenge of integrating three cultures, we have provided more services than we did aggregately previously, and we have done so at lower cost."

In the Spiral of Development

Tempting though it might be to swear allegiance to one metaphor, the twenty-five site visits provided support for a much more pliable view of organizational growth and decline. Many organizations did age up the spiral by obtaining experience and growth but some aged downward by expanding too far. Some organizations did compete against others for survival, but many also found great strength in collaboration. And most organizations did build structure and systems as they advanced upward, but some also dismantled structure and systems as they worked to innovate and learn.

More important, no matter what metaphor they used, most described their organization as moving through some kind of developmental process. Based on a careful reading of their annual reports, strategic plans, tax statements, program evaluations, and websites, as well as seventy-three interviews with board members, executive directors, and senior staff, all twenty-five organizations had reached the enterprising stage at some point in their history, seventeen had moved up to the intentional stage (leaving eight behind), nine had moved up to the robust landing (leaving another eight behind), and three had reached the reflective landing (leaving six behind).

Looking for Differences

This sample size was much too small to draw absolute conclusions about how organizations move up and down the spiral. Moreover, the twenty-five organizations were handpicked to feature variety, not similarity. Hence the sample included social service agencies and environmental advocacy groups, international relief organizations, homeless shelters, a children's museum, a circus, and AIDS nutrition groups.

Diverse as the sample was, further analysis provides more than enough comparability about the spiral of nonprofit development. According to their responses to the 2001 *Pathways to Nonprofit Excellence* survey, eight of the twenty-five had budgets under $1 million, seven had budgets from $1 million to $10 million, and ten had budgets over $10 million. Four of the twenty-five were both young (seven years old or younger) and small (under $1 million), five were young, but larger (over $1 million), four were middle aged (between seven and fifteen years old) and small, two were middle aged and larger, and ten were older (more than fifteen years old) and larger.[5]

As the following pages show, the developmental spiral helps to explain how the twenty-five organizations managed their environment, structured their internal operations, defined their leadership, recruited and managed their boards, and built their internal systems. However, I believe that all twenty-five were high performing. Although some were high performing in spite of significant organizational weaknesses, all had plenty of cause to accept their nomination as an exemplary organization.

Thus when asked whether the *Pathways* respondents were right to have been nominated for participation in a study of high-performing nonprofits, the Girl Scouts talked about its 316 local chapters and the 4 million girls it reached, Second Helpings talked about the amount of food it had rescued and graduation rates among its chefs-in-training; Environmental Defense talked about its growth from forty-five employees to 265; the San Diego Opera talked about growing from a $3 million to a $13 million company and having a balanced budget for eighteen straight years; Pact talked about growing from "an organization with zero funding, zero staff, zero anything to an organization with a national presence touching 8,000–10,000 people a year."

Once past the indicators of activity, however, most of the twenty-five focused on their basic mission. "I think we're highly accountable and never satisfied with what we've achieved," said a senior executive at Chicago's Heartland Alliance. "And we seem to be consistently asking the questions, 'How do we do better?' 'What do we have to do differently?' So, it's that 'yes, but' answer. Yes, I think we're a high-performing organization, but I think we have to be even more high performing." Moreover, as this executive argued, growth is a very shallow measure of performance:

To me, high performance is always a mix of qualitative and quantitative factors. Expansion just by virtue of doing more programs or having a larger budget is not necessarily a sign of organizational effectiveness or even organizational growth. It can be a measure of failure. It's "What are the qualitative underpinnings behind quantitative growth?" "What are our outcomes as a result of that growth?" "Are we just touching people's lives or helping to achieve change in people's lives?" That's the difference. I mean, one can greatly expand the number of lives you touch, but do nothing else, and that, to me, is not effectiveness.

The cofounder of Pact made a similar jump from the statistics to the mission. "I'd like to have people measure our programs by sustaining the consciousness of the effort. We've been able to start from zero and move outward by sustaining a consciousness about our basic mission—serving kids comes first. And when we haven't had money to do it, we've found another way."

All twenty-five organizations were not high performing naturally, however. Some were struggling to make ends meet, and others were facing extraordinary pressure. By my count, eight of the twenty-five were high performing *in spite* of their organizational infrastructure, five of which were at the enterprising landing of the spiral, and three were at the intentional stage. Robust and reflective nonprofits climb the spiral in part by making it easier to perform. Enterprising and intentional organizations often ask their employees to work miracles: they are significantly less likely to have the basic management systems in place and often move from crisis to crisis as they struggle to advance.

All twenty-five organizations were not consistently high performing, either. Several of the enterprising-intentional organizations were reeling from a budget or leadership crisis and were highly vulnerable to the post–September 11 drop in funding.

Tree Musketeers, a youth-led environmental advocacy organization located in Los Angeles, was particularly hard-hit in 2001, a year that started with federal funding cuts for environmental protection, continued with the California energy crisis, and ended with September 11. "We were having an awful financial year anyway and then September 11th happened and virtually everything dried up," said one of the organization's leaders. "You know, the small individual contributions that normally come in at the end of the year didn't come, and we were trying to keep our heads above water. We were living and breathing for that year to end, but it hasn't come back to life yet, so we're still having a bit of a struggle."

The Impact of Organizational Age and Size

Given all the patterns in this book, it should come as no surprise that organizational age and size are both related, albeit imperfectly, to movement up and down the spiral of nonprofit development. Growth generates organizational slack, which in turn begets more growth. Growth is no guarantee of organizational capacity, however. As already noted, Share Our Strength grew rapidly over the past twenty years but only recently began to invest in needed administrative infrastructure. Recall that its mission has long been getting the money out the door.

As a general rule, however, age and size do matter to organizational movement up and down the spiral. Of the twelve organizations that were both older and larger, I placed three at the intentional landing, six at the robust landing, and three at the reflective landing. Of the four that were young and small, I placed three at the enterprising and one at the intentional landing. Of the five that were young and medium to large, I placed one at the enterprising, two at the intentional, and two at the robust landing. In short, age and size do have some influence on where organizations end up in the spiral at a given point in time. No older, larger organization was enterprising, and no younger, smaller organization was reflective.

The question, of course, is what causes what. Do age and size cause movement upward, or does movement upward allow survival and growth? The answer is almost certainly a mix of cause and effect. Younger organizations face greater threats to survival, while larger organizations have more resources to invest in infrastructure. As the executive director of one of the larger organizations explained,

> I was thirty years old at the time when the organization started looking for a new leader. I guess I was interviewed by twenty-two people, the last one being the chairman of the board. He told me that I impressed a lot of people, but that there were a lot of candidates who had already run a national organization. Then he asked me how I could really expect that I'd be able to take the reigns of one of the major national organizations at my age. I just promised that I would do something about my age everyday I was on the job. And I have for the last eighteen years.

Yet aging is not quite the immutable force that experts sometimes suggest. Young organizations often behave older than they are, even as older organizations search for the fountain of bureaucratic youth. Moreover, organizations can and do alter their age and size through a host of improvement efforts, including reorganization, downsizing, leadership change, generational succession, and other forms of organizational plastic surgery, so to speak. In fact, becoming robust and reflective increases the odds that an organization can reverse the biological clock.

More important for understanding the developmental spiral, organizations can certainly do something about their growth. Of the eleven organizations that said they had experienced rapid growth in their budget, four were at the enterprising landing, one at the intentional, four at the robust, and two at the reflective; of the eleven that had experienced moderate growth, four were at the enterprising landing, five at the intentional, one at the robust, and one at the reflective.

Increased demand for services is also a weak predictor of placement on the spiral. Seventeen of the twenty-five said they had experienced significant growth in demand for services over the past years, of which seven were at the enterprising, three at the intentional, five at the robust, and two at the reflective landing. However, five of the eight organizations that reported slower growth in demand were at the intentional landing, which is exactly what one might expect. Whether by choice or because markets change, intentional organizations do, indeed, slow down somewhat.

In short, organizations may work on aging every day and clearly get bigger as they move through the enterprising stage; they do have some influence on their growth and demand for services. Despite its success in organizing the living wage campaign in Santa Monica, the Los Angeles Alliance for a New Economy did not expect to grow much in the coming five years. Asked what they might look like in 2007, an executive said, "I don't think it is really sustainable to be much bigger than we are. So maybe we will max out at twenty-five staff, $2 million, or something like that. I think we will be doing a lot more on the state level, working on policy, organizing, creating more of a network. . . . We have already slowed substantially. We had monumental growth from 1996 to 2001, when we went from between three and four staff to between sixteen and seventeen."

Comparing Environments

The twenty-five organizations had very different relationships with their environment. Although comparisons of the enterprising-intentional nonprofits with their robust-reflective peers suggest a number of interesting differences, the sample size was too small to claim statistical significance except in the presence of huge differences in the range of 40–50 percent. Based on observations during the site visits or their responses to the 2001 *Pathways* survey:

—The enterprising-intentional organizations were more likely to engage in more collaboration with other organizations: 81 percent said they collaborated to a great extent, compared with 57 percent of their robust-reflective peers.

—The enterprising-intentional organizations were twice as likely to rely on volunteers to deliver at least some of their services, in part because they had fewer employees: on average, the enterprising-intentional organizations had seventy-five employees and nearly 900 volunteers, while the robust-reflective organizations had 1,900 employees and 650 volunteers.

—The enterprising-intentional organizations were less likely to have a diversified funding base: 45 percent relied on diversified funding to a large extent, compared with 67 percent of their robust-reflective peers.

—Both sets of organizations were equally likely to have a strategic plan, but the enterprising-intentional plans were older: 29 percent of the plans at the enterprising-intentional organizations were three to five years old, while all of the plans at the robust-reflective organizations had been revised in the last year.

—All twenty-five organizations had websites, but the enterprising-intentional organizations were somewhat less likely to update their site regularly and much less likely to be able to accept contributions online: only 44 percent of the enterprising-intentional organizations could take online contributions, for example, compared with 78 percent of their robust-reflective peers.

Alongside these differences, both sets of organizations were equally likely to survey their clients regularly regarding programs and services, to pay attention to general trends in their local, national, or international environment, and to take advantage of opportunities for growth. In a sense, they were all preparing to accept miracles. "We all make our luck," said an executive with OMB Watch, a good-government advocacy group. "Or maybe a better way to put it is that we have to position ourselves to seize the opportunity when lucky situations come about. We have to have proposals ready, be ready to engage the policy fights, be ready and knowledgeable about a range of issues. Maybe I'm being cavalier, but the luck comes from other people respecting the work we do. The timing of it is fortuitous, which I call luck."

The most significant differences up and down the spiral involved strategic planning. Although almost all of the twenty-five organizations had a strategic plan, the enterprising-intentional organizations clearly devoted more energy to the effort. If not quite a fear of planning at the enterprising-intentional stage, there were concerns about costs, readiness, and implementation. Simply put, enterprising-intentional organizations worried that they simply could not afford to plan.

Consider Pact as an example. Having grown steadily over its first decade, Pact finally mustered the energy to launch its first strategic planning process in 2001. The question is not why Pact eventually decided to plan, however. As one board member explained the effort, "I think it is symptomatic of the fact that the board recognizes that this organization in its growth has tried to do so many different things and tried to do them very well that it stretched very thin. We're on the verge of what could be exponential growth, which either will be great or will kill us, and we're not looking for death here."

Rather, the question is why Pact avoided strategic planning for so long. Another board member pointed to more pressing needs: "We needed the infrastructure. We needed to get what I call an operational plan before we get the strategic plan: How are we going to run this organization really efficiently? How can we tweak what we're doing? What do we need to do to get additional dollars so we can be here next year? What we need to do now is to start planning for this into the future rather than working on a day-to-day basis."

The story was repeated time after time among the enterprising nonprofits in particular. Much as they want to be strategic, enterprising nonprofits have to be tactical to survive. For example, they said, "When your organization is in rescue mode, a strategic plan is kind of nice but won't fix your problems. It is like you want to be flying at 30,000 feet, but you're stuck on the ground." Or "If things are bleeding, it is not the time to look five years in the future. You have to figure out if you are going to survive until tomorrow."

Enterprising nonprofits must shepherd their time and energy wisely. Done well, strategic planning can create new opportunities for growth; done poorly, it can become drudgery. As a senior executive at Pillsbury United Communities remembered its first strategic planning effort, "It seemed like we were just restating a lot of stuff that we had already talked about. We didn't seem to be moving anywhere, didn't seem to crystallize. The big question was really what path we wanted to take, but that never seemed to get put up front and center. We talked about every-thing but that."

But as Pillsbury learned, planning is just like any other organizational skill: practice matters. "I think we're more aware of how we carry out the strategic plan," said another senior executive of more recent plans. "It's not just something that you put in a drawer. You have to deliver on it, evaluate it, and take the time to assess whether it's still relevant. I think we're more intentional about those kinds of things."

Expensive though it may be, strategic planning helped many of the intentional, robust, and reflective organizations to move up the devel-opment spiral. "I think a strategic plan is really important," said a sen-ior executive at Lakefront Supportive Housing. "We just adopted a ten-year outcome plan for the organization. But it is not the first thing that I'd do if I were trying to improve basic performance. The first thing I'd do is raise money. When I came in, I raised money from every source I could. I had to get a certain amount of support to build an infrastruc-ture for the organization. Once I had that infrastructure, which took me two to three years, then I could think about strategic planning. Starting from scratch, strategic planning may not be critical, but it's critical pretty soon."

For robust-reflective organizations, strategic planning is often part of everyday organizational life, even a way of thinking. According to a sen-ior executive at Heartland Alliance,

> Our strategic planning process is extremely strong. It's taken very seriously. It includes input from outside people, clients, the board, from all levels of program management. We also have something called the Program Cabinet, which is composed of the senior direc-tors who pretty much cover all areas. We meet monthly; the exec-utive team meets monthly; our controllers meet quarterly not only with the executive officers but with all of the different program directors to talk about financial implications. We also have special task force working groups that meet, including our information technology group. There is a very strong mandate to make sure that input on the mission comes from above as well as to make sure that once the mission has been determined, it flows throughout the organization.

A second executive described the process as anything but easy. "We do client focus groups, staff focus groups, surveys, all that kind of stuff every year at the beginning of the strategic planning process. The planning process starts at the bottom and then trickles back down again at the end. Sometimes it feels very burdensome, you know. It's a big process that we go through every year; it's part of our life from December to June, and then we're planning for the next year."

Comparing Structures

The spiral of organizational development clearly works its will through organizational structure, as does age and size. As the following list suggests, being enterprising or intentional brings agility and risk:

—The sixteen enterprising-intentional nonprofits were flatter than their nine peers: 63 percent reported two or fewer layers between the top and bottom of their organization, compared with just 33 percent of their robust-reflective peers. Conversely, 67 percent of the robust-reflective organizations had at least four layers between the top and bottom, compared with just 13 percent of their enterprising-intentional peers, easily one of the most statistically significant differences among these comparisons.

—The enterprising-intentional organizations reported much less difficulty holding onto employees and volunteers, in part because they were flatter and therefore could offer more opportunities for challenging work. Just 38 percent reported any difficulty at all retaining staff, compared with 67 percent of the robust-reflective organizations, and even fewer (19 percent) said it was not at all difficult retaining volunteers, compared with 33 percent of their robust-reflective peers.

—The enterprising-intentional organizations reported less access to discretionary resources. Just six of the sixteen said they had a cash reserve of any size at the time of the site visits, compared with all but one of their nine robust-reflective peers; just one reported a permanent endowment of any size, compared with six of their robust-reflective peers, and just one had any kind of innovation investment fund, compared with three of their robust-reflective peers.

—The enterprising-intentional organizations reported more difficulty retaining leaders: 75 percent reported some or great difficulty retaining leaders, compared with 56 percent of their robust-reflective peers.

Both sets of organizations were equally likely to report that staff often worked in teams, to say that staff and management were comfortable taking risks and open to new ideas, and to delegate routine decisions to frontline employees.

Not surprising, the site visits revealed very different levels of organizational strength. Many of the enterprising-intentional organizations were still making program-administrative trade-offs as they sought to establish themselves or focus old programs. As one of the cofounders of Pact argued, "I don't feel it's been a mistake for us to focus our first ten years primarily on honing our services and our mission and focusing on our program. I think it was important to really understand who we were and to define that in a clear way. And there just were no staff and not enough time in our twenty-four-hour days to respond to what we needed."

Obviously, Pact had different needs than, say, Care, the Girl Scouts, or the Nature Conservancy. "I think we've been good at asking for help," said a Pact executive. "I don't know if that's true of all heads of nonprofits or not. We haven't wasted a lot of our time reinventing the wheel. It's always been our first instinct to ask somebody. We never try to do it ourselves when we have no clue. I mean, we didn't know how to do a budget."

The Girl Scouts of America is a perfect counterpoint. Not only was the organization much farther up the spiral structurally, but it had its own in-house consulting firm to help its 316 member organizations improve. Created in 1997, the unit had a staff of eighty and an annual budget of $7 million. Its sole purpose was to build capacity across the range of high-to-low performers by raising the bar across the 316 member organizations, while reducing the "tail" of the distribution through cooperative mergers and occasional takeovers.

The unit had a special team that worked with particularly troubled councils. As a senior staffer explained, "They can take an enormous amount of time from the staff. So we have a team at large that will take councils into intensive care for a period of time. It's composed of people who have the greatest chance of making a huge improvement in an eighteen-month period, and it has worked to some degree." Asked how the unit created momentum for change in the absence of strong sanctions, she focused on mission and measurement:

I think that we have in general a lot of people who really care about the mission. So you can motivate them by some objective data showing that they are not necessarily achieving what they might. And one of the things that has really helped us as we have begun to harness the power of computers is that we now provide information to every council. Actually we are now providing it every year, but it used to be that we did it when we first started. I am going to say that this is over the last five or six years, not very long. But we provide them a very detailed set of maps of their geography: of where the population lives and where the Girl Scout population is and what percentage of the available girls they are serving in each of their various communities or racial groups. Or we even give a profile of the median income by zip code. They can really take a look at that and say, "Here is where we are doing well; here is where we are doing not so well" and set objective targets.

Whereas organic and enterprising organizations may need basic engineering to move up the developmental spiral, robust and reflective organizations may need reengineering, streamlining, and more aggressive planning. At Care, for example, the global campaign against poverty involved two very different planning efforts. The first involved internal structure and systems, while the second turned to the mission itself. "The first strategic plan was more inward looking," a senior executive explained. "That is, we were trying to increase our fund-raising, build up our systems and our structures, and make us more effective within. Programmatically, we had changes going on, but the second strategic plan was much more outward looking. It was more concerned with how we were interacting with the world and what we were contributing to the world rather than focusing inwardly on our structures."

Asked how Care avoids complacency from its perch as one of the nation's most visible organizations, this executive said, "We'll never run out of things to make us a better organization. It all goes back to mission and to core values. I think there needs to be broadly felt excitement and commitment, and it needs to be alive. We start off every board meeting reading our vision statement. Our chairman reads it, and people listen and think about it."

For Care, staying focused also involved succession planning, the organization's first early retirement program to reduce its size, a Care Academy to train new staff, and a new logo, all of which underpinned the organization's new mission as a place "where the end of poverty begins." As one senior executive explained the logo, "We got away from the block letters and went to lower case so people would stop thinking of Care as an acronym. We got away from the earth tones. We got away from the more corporate reds, blue, green, primary color look and went to something that was more compatible with the work that we do in the field. And we came up with hands that actually form a circle. Different people see different things in it. The only challenge, of course, was that everybody is an expert when it comes to colors and words."[6]

Comparing Leadership

Whether by choice or default, organizations need different kinds of leadership as they move up the development spiral. Organizations that start out with passionate, entrepreneurial, even autocratic leaders may eventually need a more participatory, team-oriented approach. According to the organizational histories collected during the site visits, the twenty-five high-performing nonprofits changed directions several times as they moved upward toward the robust-reflective landing.

—The enterprising-intentional nonprofits were more likely to be led by charismatic leaders: nine of the sixteen leaders I met at the enterprising-intentional nonprofits had what I define as a charismatic style, compared with just three of the nine leaders of their robust-reflective peers.

—The enterprising-intentional organizations were much more likely to be led by their founder: nine of the sixteen organizations were headed by their founder(s), compared with none of the robust-reflective organizations. The enterprising-intentional organizations were much less likely to have an executive team at the top of the organization, in part because they were smaller and in part because they were flatter.

—The executive directors of the enterprising-intentional organizations assigned greater importance to growth and expansion than their peers: asked which of six words were most important for describing a high-performing nonprofit, 50 percent of the enterprising-intentional executives chose the words innovative, collaborative, or entrepreneurial, while 66 percent of the robust-reflective executives chose the words principled, rigorous, or resilient.

—The executive directors of the enterprising-intentional organizations were far less likely to use business language to describe their leadership philosophy: 44 percent of the leaders of enterprising-intentional organizations used business language such as customers, benchmarking, total quality management, products, and continuous improvement at some point during the site visit interviews, compared with 89 percent of the leaders of robust-reflective organizations.

It is tempting to attribute many of these differences to the high number of founders among the enterprising-intentional organizations. After all, as a board member at Second Helpings described the needs of her intentional organization, "Founder-led organizations are a curious lot, as you know. Sometimes they can become quite inwardly focused. The founder has the vision, and she is almost maniacal about it. More than sometimes, you find the founder saying, 'If you build it, they will come.' There is a wonderful spiritual dimension to it, but also a belief that things will take care of themselves. This organization feels like a post-founder organization a bit. It is more disciplined."

Moreover, there is some evidence that founders have very different views of organizational life. Organizations headed by their founders were less likely to have a strategic plan and less likely to pay attention to the plan they had; they were less likely to have an executive team at the top of the organization; their fund-raising was affected more by the September 11 terrorist attacks; their boards met less frequently but were more likely to include clients; they had at least some accounting weaknesses, fewer performance reviews, fewer job descriptions in the file, fewer systems for measuring work activities, and no system for measuring outcomes. The founders were also much more likely to stick around: seven of the nine founders had been in their job more than ten years, compared with just six of the sixteen non-founders.

As always, the question is what causes what. Do founders create weaker boards to insulate themselves, or do enterprising-intentional organizations start out with weaker boards? Do founders eschew outcomes measurement to protect their vision, or do enterprising-intentional organizations have problems developing good indicators? Do founders focus so much on vision that they ignore internal structure and systems, or do enterprising-intentional organizations struggle to develop infrastructure?

The answer is almost certainly a mix of both. Founders bring great strength and commitment to their work but may neglect core systems in favor of the mission; enterprising-intentional organizations have problems building infrastructure and recruiting strong boards.

Moreover, like the founders at the enterprising-intentional organizations, the non-founders at the robust-reflective organizations often reported the same difficulties that the founders did. As the executive director of a robust organization recalled her hiring, "The previous CEO's eyes were much bigger than his pockets. The expansion had been done very quickly without the money to sustain it and without the internal infrastructure to hold it together. There was a disconnect between the

CEO and the chief financial officer, and the board didn't get the information it needed. The CEO was just out there on his own. We had a very wonderful vision, but vision isn't worth one cent if you can't back it up."

Her colleague at a performing arts organization had a nearly identical experience. "I was one of fifty applicants for the job. I have since learned that I was the only one who asked for budgets. I analyzed the data and said it just didn't make sense." Referring to the use of free tickets to create the illusion of demand, this executive director remarked, "There was so much paper in the house that people were scared to light a match. Too many arts institutions think it's all about Mickey Rooney and Judy Garland saying, 'Let's put on a show. I've got some curtains, and my father has a barn.' It's not like that."

Like the founders of enterprising-intentional organizations, the leaders of the robust-reflective organizations also worked hard to learn their job. As the head of one of the largest organizations in the sample reflected, "Most of the organizations that I had led before coming here were small organizations. I could get my arms around them—you know, somewhere between twenty-five, thirty, and seventy people total. I had a lot to learn about managing and leading a large organization and had a lot of on-the-job-training with regard to building the systems and structures and communication flows that go with this organization."

Yet even as they worried about repairing damage and learning their job, the leaders of the nine robust-reflective organizations tended to focus more broadly on challenging their organization to aim higher. Asked why Care launched a painful strategic planning process in 1996, a senior executive explained, "We needed to become a more explicitly principled organization." Asked why his screen saver featured the word "inspire," another executive said he was his organization's "chief visionary officer." Finally, asked why the senior staff of the Indianapolis Children's Museum worked so hard to change the organization's mission to declare its intent "to transform the lives of children and their families," a senior executive simply said, "You've got to sustain it, and you've got to keep measuring it, and you've got to keep tweaking it along the way."

Environmental Defense provides a particularly potent example of how leadership approaches change over time. The organization clearly moved upward from the enterprising to the intentional landing in the middle to late 1980s, moved up again to robustness in the early 1990s, and reached the reflective stage by the early 2000s. Although Fred Krupp was the executive director through the four "epochs," as he described them, his

leadership clearly aged into a different style that included more delegation, greater focus, and a. recognition that he could not do everything by
himself.

The most visible sign was his decision to hire a deputy director for
programs, ceding to another executive responsibility for the basic science
and advocacy that underpins Environmental Defense's mission, while
acknowledging that the organization had grown too large for a flat leadership structure. "Fred couldn't possibly manage the hands-on management and do all of the other things he had to do in order for the
organization to grow," said a senior executive of the new position. "His
highest and best use was to think about strategic opportunities and
efforts, not to manage the programs. The organization had grown significantly and required more management than it had."

In turn, the new leadership structure created momentum toward
greater internal accountability. "Environmental Defense used to view the
ideal staff person as a ranger riding off into the sunset to do justice for
the environment," said another executive. "There is still an inherent
egalitarian belief that people should develop their own agendas, but people have come to believe that further management is needed. There is
always a tension between management and independence, a tension
between headquarters and field offices, but the organization became
steadily more strategic, in part by merging programs and reducing the
number of direct reports to the director."

The restructuring prompted a round of intense sorting. "Large-scale
planning efforts aren't things that anyone finds hugely enjoyable," said
the executive, "but it forced us to examine what other groups were doing,
what other groups thought of us, what other people thought was our
competitive advantage. And it helped us to decide that there were two
areas where we had a real core strength: global warming and biodiver-
sity. And it led us to adopt two other issues that few other national organizations were focusing on at the time: oceans and environmental health."

The strategic planning prompted further organizational development,
including more marketing power and better use of technology. "We had
been using a lot of technology, but had nobody who was able to make
rational judgments about what makes sense. You can get sucked into
spending large amounts of money if you don't know what you are doing,
so we hired someone to be our chief technology person and bulked up
our finance unit. We are more disciplined, more transparent, and more

outcomes-oriented today than we were a decade ago." Asked just what motivated all the change, this executive simply replied, "It was just Fred, who wasn't getting any sleep because he was trying to do everything. He had no help either on the administrative side—managing the budget and fund-raising—or on the program side."

One final point is worth sharing before comparing boards. The robust-reflective organizations were much more likely to embrace business language to describe their work. "It is like running a business! It is like running a business!" said a senior executive at Vital Bridges (Open Hand Chicago), when asked about her greatest leadership challenge. "You need to have financial integrity and accountability. You need to have good marketing and engage people in the use of your product and in buying that product for the donors and corporations. You need to have a good human resource system for paid and unpaid personnel that rewards high performance and engages people in improving their performance. And you need to have leadership that makes it happen."

These leaders were clearly aware that using business language had its limits, however. "Nonprofits often reject what we regard as a more corporate or colder and impersonal way of looking at the world," said a senior executive at the Nature Conservancy. "So there is some push back when you use terms like 'customers' and 'products.' That sounds calculated and cold and corporate and impersonal. So you have to put it in a more comfortable language."

An executive at the Heartland Alliance echoed this sentiment. "We've often been reminded that we're not a business, that we're an organization that does good. How can you really have meaningful productivity standards if you're being responsive to human beings? We say that we should use benchmarking and the best management tools available but segue into warmer terminology because of our stewardship. It's a stewardship responsibility that requires good business practice."

For the Big Apple Circus, being business-like was essential to remaining nonprofit-like. The organization had to be highly effective against big competitors such as Barnum and Bailey and Cirque de Soleil, but it also had a nonprofit mission. "We are in the show business," an executive argued. "You are only as good as your last show. And believe me, I would have the greatest job in the world if we didn't have to create a new show every year, but we do. Our audience is not going to come back and see the same show."

Comparing Boards

Leadership involves more than the executive director. It also involves boards, employees, clients, and communities. Defined broadly, organizations can strengthen their leadership in many ways. They can include clients on their board, collaborate with other organizations inside and outside their field, delegate authority to their employees, work in teams, and build their strategic plan from the bottom up, not the top down.

At the board level, all twenty-five organizations in the sample did at least something to strengthen their board. However, whereas the enterprising-intentional organizations often struggled to build their basic board structure, robust-reflective organizations worked to deepen expertise and tighten boundaries.

—The enterprising-intentional organizations had greater difficulty recruiting and retaining board members: just 38 percent reported no difficulty in doing so, compared with 89 percent of their robust-reflective peers.

—The entrepreneurial-intentional organizations were less likely to describe their board as understanding their general duties, their role in setting policy, or their role in overseeing the organization's performance: 56 percent described their board as understanding each of these three roles very well, compared with 89 percent of their robust-reflective peers.

Both sets of organizations were equally likely to have an executive committee on their board, to have subcommittees, and to meet regularly. However, there is no question that boards evolve with their organizations. At the Ancona School, for example, the board moved from sweat and tears to strategic planning. "We're no longer talking to our executive director about how to make sure that the day-to-day things are done or to critique her on her day-to-day things. I don't think that anyone comes in and does that or wants to do that. But that has changed. The school was started by parents who came in and painted the walls and chose the tile for the floor. Those days are gone. There has been an evolution from a hands-on board to becoming strategic planners. It takes time for that change to evolve."

A board member at Calvary Women's Services told a similar story. "Past boards worked very hard at things like the Jingle Bell Ball, which is a major fund-raiser, but it was short-term thinking about how to bring in money as opposed to asking whether this is the kind of event we should do. Is it going to bring in people who are going to then feel somehow connected to the shelter? Are they going to be giving money because they care about homeless issues in D.C. and are going to want to volunteer then? We're trying to do more strategic thinking about the shelter itself and how we connect people to it."

Sometimes, boards evolve through crisis. At Open Hand Chicago, the financial meltdown led to a complete overhaul of board governance. "We met with the board right after the CEO left and laid it all out," said one executive. "Here is the debt. Here are the payables. Here is what we can do. Here is what we must do very quickly. And they said, 'Go do it.' And we said, 'Fine, but what are you going to do about yourself? You weren't watching.' There's no one left from that board today."

Other times, boards evolve through practice and learning. "When we started out, we were micro-managing to some extent," said a board member of Second Helpings. "So we had to learn how to wear multiple hats as board members. We have board members that volunteer in the kitchen, for example. When they are in the kitchen, they are just volunteers, not board members. We decided to create job descriptions for board members to keep things straight."

Whatever the driver, boards either change with their organization or get changed by it. The board of the Indianapolis Children's Museum had its own strategic planning process, as did the boards of several other robust-reflective organizations. "We look at our strengths as a board, our weaknesses, who we need, what we need to change," said one board member. "We hold ten meetings a year with two retreats: one about how we do our work, the other a blue-sky retreat on just about anything we want. And every board meeting has a Board Development Moment, when we just stop and focus for five minutes on anything *but* the financials, or the personnel process, or the next exhibit."

Comparing Systems

The board is a logical segue itself into discussions of management systems, for it is both a source of leadership and a management system. It can also be a strong advocate for or opponent of organizational capacity building. As such, at least some of the differences described below involve board-level resistance to internal investment:

—The enterprising-intentional organizations put less emphasis on technology: they were less likely than their robust-reflective peers to say that their information technology was very adequate and less able to generate up-to-date and accurate financial information. Only 25 percent of the enterprising-intentional organizations had what I describe as a strong accounting system, compared with all but one of the robust-reflective organizations.

—The enterprising-intentional organizations were less likely to have a pay-for-performance system, annual performance reviews for their employees, or formal job descriptions: just 25 percent had a pay-for-performance system, 44 percent had annual performance reviews, and 31 percent had job descriptions. By comparison, 44 percent of the robust-reflective organizations had a pay-for-performance system, 56 percent had annual performance reviews, and 67 percent had job descriptions.

—Although both sets of organizations were equally likely to have health insurance for their employees, the enterprising-intentional organizations were somewhat less likely to provide any kind of pension plan and were significantly less likely to provide life insurance and disability insurance for their employees: only 31 percent offered life insurance, and just 25 percent offered disability insurance, while 78 percent of the robust-reflective organizations offered both benefits.

—The enterprising-intentional organizations were less likely to use objective data in making management or program decisions: just 44 percent said they used such data, compared with 89 percent of their robust-reflective peers.

—The enterprising-intentional organizations knew less about both their activities and outcomes: just 50 percent had a system for measuring work activities such as number of people served, meals delivered, repeat visitors, and so forth, and just 19 percent were trying to measure program outcomes. By comparison, all nine of the robust-reflective organizations had strong work measurement systems, and 56 percent had at least some outcome measures.

—Both sets of organizations were equally likely to provide funding for staff training. However, when asked how much funding they dedicated to training, just 19 percent of the enterprising-intentional organizations said they provided "a lot" of funding, compared with 44 percent of their robust-reflective peers.

Despite these differences in training and benefits, both sets of organizations reported little difficulty recruiting and retaining staff, perhaps suggesting that enterprising-intentional organizations compensate by giving frontline employees more responsibility through their relatively flat internal structure.

These comparisons suggest just how far enterprising-intentional organizations must go to build the infrastructure for sustainable high performance. Organizations can muddle through with many weaknesses, but not with leaky financial systems and poor internal measurement. They cannot know the true cost of anything they do if they do not have a decent accounting package and cannot calculate efficiency and productivity without hard measures of what they do. They cannot let the paper clips take over, but neither can they survive without strong systems for tracking what they spend and how they spend it, thereby creating a double bottom line that measures both their financial progress and social impact.

These systems also make high performance both possible and natural. "I think this organization had developed the programmatic skills and reputation to be a national exemplar seven or eight years ago," said one senior staffer at the Heartland Alliance, "but we did not have a strong accounting package or technology team. I think there's a reticence among nonprofits to putting money into those areas. But the fact that we did make the commitment to upgrade our computers, our phones, and our accounting system is now paying off in tremendous dividends. These systems pay for themselves very quickly. I mean, I can remember when we all had 286s and didn't have voice mail."

As the list of differences shows, few of the twenty-five had been able to develop strong outcome measures that might lead to firm estimates of the social rate of return on investment. But many were working on the issue. As an intentional organization working its way upward, Chicago's Ancona School was struggling to master the measurement issue, a task made all the more difficult by its Montessori roots. "The test scores don't measure anything important to me," said a senior teacher of her organization's effort to increase its sophistication. "If a kid can write a great essay, I'm thrilled. If a kid can persuade somebody on something, I'm thrilled. If a kid can organize other kids to do a project, I'm thrilled. I have high standards, but I don't know that we have a good set of benchmarks for measuring or assessing every student. The problem is that standardized measurement has always been a contradiction with our emphasis on the individual child."

Friends of the Chicago River faced a similar challenge as it worked up from the enterprising to the intentional landing. "I think that as the river has improved over the twenty-two years since this organization was founded, what we need to be telling about it also has evolved," said a senior staffer of the challenges in measuring the impact of an advocacy organization. "They used to put bleach in the Chicago River because that is how they treated sewage. When the sewers would overflow, you were killing all the stuff in the river with the bleach. Well, they cut that out in 1987. Nobody has to get up in arms about that anymore because it is done and it is over. So it is an evolution of the way that the river is being used and treated. We are moving along in sync with that at the same time that we are doing policy and planning."

Even robust-reflective organizations can struggle to develop good outcome measures, however. Although Lakefront Supportive Housing knew a great deal about its residents, including job placement rates, a senior executive acknowledged, "We haven't done a systematic analysis of measuring whether or not a person is making progress, particularly when we're trying to be very client focused. We don't want to use a cookie-cutter model and don't want to say, 'Everybody's got to do this or that.'"

In a similar vein, the Indianapolis Children's Museum knew a great deal about its visitors, including the number of repeat visits and overall satisfaction, but continued to develop better measures of its ability to transform the lives of children and families. "We know that childhood continues to shrink," said a senior executive. "We know that family time, quality time continue to shrink, and there are few places where you can take your family and not only spend time together, but learn." The museum is struggling to figure out ways of measuring the experience in something other than costs and has started to measure itself against both nonprofit and profit-making educational and entertainment organizations to develop more advanced measures.

Even when an organization has deep information on both activities (for example, number of people served) and outputs (for example, number of return visits), it is still difficult, if not impossible, to measure outcomes. The challenge is clear in the Heartland Alliance's health care program, which served 11,000 poor people in 2003, 8,500 of whom were homeless. "We're not at all where I want us to be as far as looking at what we're doing for the people that we're serving," said a senior program executive.

We do look at pregnancy outcomes, which is a great outcome measure for a health care organization. We also have a pretty sophisticated outcome measurement system for our 300 HIV patients. But I don't know how well we're taking care of diabetics;

I don't know how well we're taking care of people with hypertension; I don't know how well we're taking care of people who come into the clinic and are sent off into another health care system somewhere. Are we getting information back? Are we getting the patient back? Are we continuing to monitor their care? What happens after somebody goes into the hospital? We don't have any information on that person unless he or she happens to show up on our doorstep in six months or a year. I would really like to dig down to the next level.

Measurement is not an end in itself, of course. It is merely a rigorous means to ask the core questions that brought an organization into being in the first place: How will we make a difference? Who does what? Why do we exist? And how will we know we are successful, if we are? Organizations that invent the answers often find themselves staring up at their past success, wondering what went wrong.

Capacity Building for Advancement

Robust-reflective organizations do not reach the higher landings overnight. Some move a step or two each year, passing through the landings in a nearly linear fashion, while others accelerate for a time, hold steady, then accelerate again. However, all confront inevitable surprises along the way: a leadership crisis, a budget shortfall, a failed program, a financial meltdown. Robust-reflective organizations are very good at what they do, but they are not practically perfect in every way. They make mistakes, hire bad employees, recruit apathetic board members, overreach, and underperform.

There is no guarantee, therefore, that the robust-reflective organizations described here will remain robust-reflective ten years from now or that the enterprising-intentional organizations will rise. Everything depends on how these organizations react to the inevitable surprises and disappointments they confront along the way, whether they can demonstrate results, and how well they do in reinforcing the infrastructure for advancement. Indeed, many are already busy creating a future leadership crisis by ignoring succession planning: although more than half of the executives interviewed during the site visits had ten years or more of experience, only three of their organizations had a succession plan, oftentimes because the executive directors worried about what one executive described as "a shadow always hanging around." But the real shadow they should worry about is the future: it is uncertain and unstoppable.

Robust and reflective organizations do have one powerful advantage in remaining robust and reflective, however. They have deep experience with capacity building. They did not get to the higher landings by accident. They planned, built, expanded, focused, and measured their way upward. Although the enterprising-intentional organizations in the sample had done a great deal of capacity building, it was clearly of a different kind. At least measured by their general view of past activities, the robust-reflective organizations tended to focus more on confronting the outside world through benchmarking, standards, and greater transparency, while enterprising-intentional organizations tended to focus on building internal structures and systems.

—The enterprising-intentional organizations were less likely to benchmark against other organizations for improvement: 50 percent of the enterprising-intentional organizations said they did so, compared with 78 percent of their robust-reflective peers.

—Asked about the importance of improving various aspects of organizational life, the enterprising-intentional organizations were less likely to rate external relationships and internal systems as very important, but more likely to rate internal structure as key. Both groups put a nearly identical, and emphatic, exclamation point on improving leadership.

—Asked which of the four areas was most important to improve first, the enterprising-intentional organizations were more likely to focus on improving internal structure and less likely to focus on leadership: 25 percent said internal structure came first, compared with 11 percent of their robust-reflective peers, while 56 percent said leadership came first, compared with 78 percent of their peers.

—The enterprising-intentional organizations were less likely than their robust-reflective peers to say that their organization's performance had been improved by adopting management standards, making nonprofits more open to the public and media, and strengthening external reviews by organizations such as the Better Business Bureau's Wise Giving Alliance and GuideStar.

—The enterprising-intentional organizations were more likely than their peers to say that their organization's performance had been improved through greater collaboration, reducing overlap and duplication, strategic planning, executive training, funding for capacity building, and management assistance grants.

All of the organizations needed more funding for capacity building, although the robust-reflective organizations had more resources at their disposal (both the Girl Scouts and Lakefront Supportive Housing had their own consulting units: the former for its Girl Scout councils, the latter for other affordable housing organizations). As a senior executive at Vital Bridges noted, "Lots of funders are interested in supporting mergers once the plans are in place, and all the boards have voted to merge, but they don't acknowledge the cost of getting to that vote, which is really critical. If you do that process wrong, if you aren't rigorous enough about it, if you don't think enough, your decision could be bad. And then no matter how much money you have for integration, it is not going to work. But they have a right to fund whatever they want." Luckily, Open Hand Chicago received $60,000 from a national foundation, which was just about half of what it cost to create Vital Bridges, which offers the most comprehensive nutrition services in the nation.

All of the organizations had received funding for capacity building at one time or another, but most of it was for small initiatives here and there. It was very rare for an organization to have a longer-term relationship of the kind the Packard Foundation had with the Pacific Repertory Theater. Packard was there when the theater needed a better tent in its second year, a strategic plan in its fifth, and a new building in its eighth.

Because of their larger size and scope, the robust-reflective organizations had the greatest difficulty securing outside support for the more sophisticated capacity building they needed to maintain momentum. Heartland Alliance had to build the Intranet connecting its seventy programs by pinching pennies across the organizations; Environmental Defense conducted its annual planning entirely with inside funds; the Nature Conservancy launched its new technology system with a small grant from Packard but used "seat-cushion" money for its much larger effort to refocus its programs; and Care was only able to create its new logo with pro bono support from a national advertising agency. Perhaps that is how it should be. Robust-reflective capacity building is often so expensive that it could easily consume every last dollar of the funding available for capacity building.

Capacity building involves more than discrete projects, of course. For most of the robust-reflective organizations in the sample, it was just as much a way of thinking as a set of interventions. Hence the substantial amount of benchmarking. Although several enterprising-intentional nonprofits talked about benchmarking, including Calvary Women's Services, the robust-reflective organizations were constantly scanning their environment for new ideas. Lakefront Supportive Housing gave its chief financial officer a year's sabbatical to benchmark large real estate companies to understand how housing companies grow; the Girl Scouts benchmarked its own 316 councils to find out how to manage volunteers, develop human resource systems, and manage camps and centers; and the Indianapolis Children's Museum benchmarked everything from accounting to marketing. The point is to keep looking.

Conclusions

No matter where the organization might be in time and place, capacity building is a potentially high-yield, low-cost investment that can improve program success dramatically. The question is not whether capacity building improves capacity, but when to use it and how to improve success.

I believe the case for capacity building is strong. Although the case would be even stronger with the kind of objective evidence that could show clear before-and-after effects, there are enough independent sources to support the simple logic chain outlined in chapter 1. Capacity-building activities such as planning, reorganizing, training, and communicating lead to increased capacity measured by organizational outputs such as improved morale, focus, efficiency, and productivity, which are clearly related to better management and improved program impacts, which are linked to both employee and public perceptions of nonprofit effectiveness, which are linked to more general confidence in nonprofits, which is related to discretionary giving and volunteering. As I argue early in the book, the link between effectiveness and confidence is merely icing on the cake: the links between capacity building and organizational effectiveness are more than enough to justify further organizational investment.

I also believe the case for capacity building would be much stronger if the nonprofit sector and its funders would provide greater support for it. Although much of the capacity building covered by the 318 examples was successful, much of it was also often underfunded, underplanned, poorly tracked with hard evidence, and done with little or no contact with the outside world. Boards were underengaged, as were middle-level and frontline staff, which makes capacity building highly dependent on executive perseverance, hardly a strength of the nonprofit sector. Reading between the lines of the survey and the longer interviews, too much capacity building is done by hunch. Much as one can celebrate trial and error in many endeavors, capacity building is arguably best done when built on the lessons learned from someone else's trial and error. It may be relatively inexpensive in dollars, but not in stress or distraction.

One can also argue that nonprofits are spending too much time fixing leaky pipes and broken windows, while jumping at available funding, and not enough doing the kind of continuous improvement that prevents crises and emergencies in the first place. Although there is no single pathway to organizational excellence, nonprofits appear to do best when they get in the capacity-building habit, which in turn builds the organizational infrastructure for monitoring each successive effort.

Ultimately, successful capacity building involves an effective strategy for change, which leads back to funding, measurement, outside contact, and planning. Successful capacity building does not take nerves of steel, but it does take more than a wing and a prayer. It also works best when the intervention fits the problems. Organizations that fix every leaky pipe and broken window with duct tape may soon find themselves deluged by catastrophe. Although it is easy to blame every capacity-building failure on the change agent, I believe a very high percentage of efforts fail because the change itself does not fit the problem.

Success depends, therefore, on that sense of organizational time and place. Strategic planning may be too much for some organizations on the spiral, but not enough for others; investments in new technologies may be essential for some organizations, but a waste of resources for others. Organizations cannot know where they need to go if they do not know where they already are.

Appendix A

The Capacity-Building Survey

This appendix presents the questionnaire underlying the analysis of organizational capacity building in this book. The Internet survey was completed by 318 nonprofits, and their overall responses are reported below as percentages. The sample is discussed in detail in chapter 3.

Q1. What is your current position or title? If more than one of the following apply, please choose the one that best describes your primary role.

Administrator/chief of staff/vice president	8
Chief executive officer/president	31
Chief financial officer/treasurer	3
Executive director/associate director	44
Member of board or member at large	5
Other	8
No response	2

Q2. How many years have you served in this capacity for your organization?

Less than five years	49
Five to less than ten years	25
Ten to less than fifteen years	10
More than fifteen years	16
No response	< 1

Q3. Do you work for a local, national, or international organization?

Local organization	81
National organization	11
International organization	7
No response	1

Q4. What type of work does the nonprofit organization you work for do? Please check as many as apply.

Arts and culture	15
Environment	7
Job training or economic or community development	11
Housing/homelessness	17
Nutrition or hunger	9
Education	32
Children and youth services	31
General human services	17
Science	3
Health	21
Job training	9
Other	31
No response to all	1

Q5. How well do the following words describe the people you serve [list items were rotated]?

	Very well	Somewhat well	Not too well	Not well at all	No response
a. Low income	43	26	18	8	5
b. Disadvantaged	38	30	14	12	6
c. Diverse	47	34	12	3	4
d. Urban	34	34	13	12	6
e. Children and/or families	53	25	8	8	6

Q6. Please indicate how much change there has been in the last five years for each of the following areas [list items were rotated]. Has there been a great deal of growth, some growth, no significant change, some decline, or a great deal of decline?

	Great deal of growth	Some growth	No significant change	Some decline	Great deal of decliine	No resonse
a. Number of programs or services you offer	28	51	14	5	1	1
b. Number of clients or members you serve	34	46	9	8	2	1
c. Size of your budget	25	51	8	11	3	1

Q7. Words often have somewhat different meanings to people. What do the words "capacity building" mean to you? [Open ended.]

Q8. Please indicate whether you strongly agree, somewhat agree, somewhat disagree, or strongly disagree with each of the following statements [list items were rotated]:

	Strongly agree	Some-what agree	Some-what disagree	Strongly disagree	No response
a. An organization can be very well managed and still not achieve its program goals.	36	48	9	6	1
b. An organization can be very effective in achieving its program goals but not be well managed.	19	33	27	20	1

Q9. Thinking back over the last five years, which of the following, if any, has your organization done to improve its management or programmatic impact? Please check as many as apply.

Sought to improve its external relationships through collaboration, mergers, strategic planning, fund-raising, media relations	88
Sought to improve its internal structure through reorganization, team building, adding staff, enhancing diversity, creating a rainy day fund or reserve, creating a fund for new ideas	86
Sought to improve its leadership through board development, leadership development, succession planning, a change in leadership, greater delegation of responsibility for routine decisions	77
Sought to improve its internal management systems through new information technology, budget and accounting systems, changes in your personnel system, staff training, evaluation, organizational assessment, outcomes/results measurement	85
None	0
No response to all	> 1

Q10. Which of the following methods for improving external relationships did you use? Please check as many as apply. [Based on those who sought to improve management or programmatic impact by improving external relationships; N = 281.]

Collaboration	85
Mergers	10
Strategic planning	72
Fund-raising	65
Media relations	61
Other	13
No response to all	< 1

Q11. Which of the following methods for improving internal structure did you use? Please check as many as apply. [Based on those who sought to improve management or programmatic impact by improving internal relationships; N = 273.]

Reorganization	67
Team building	73
Addition of staff	69
Recruiting a more diverse staff	31
Creation of a rainy day fund or reserve	37
Creation of a fund for new ideas	17
Other	12
No response to all	1

Q12. Which of the following methods for improving leadership did you use? Please check as many as apply. [Based on those who sought to improve management or programmatic impact by improving leadership; N = 246.]

Board development	80
Leadership development	63
Succession planning	27
A change in leadership	45
Greater delegation of responsibility for routine decisions	67
Other	10
No response to all	< 1

Q13. Which of the following methods for improving your internal management systems did you use? Please check as many as apply. [Based on those who sought to improve management or programmatic impact by improving internal management systems; N = 269.]

New information technology	80
Accounting systems	62
Changes in personnel system	39
Staff training	75
Evaluation	60
Organizational assessment	52
Outcomes/result measurement	48
Other	6
No response to all	1

For the next few questions, please think of the effort you know best that your organization has made to improve its performance. This could be an effort that was very successful or one that was not too successful.

Q14. Please give a very brief description of this effort to improve your organization's performance. [Open ended.]

Types of efforts described were as follows:

External relations (net)	35
Collaboration/partnerships/alliances	2
Mergers	2
Strategic planning/mission	10
Fund-raising/development	4
External communications/marketing/media relations	6
Program development/redesign	6
Facility expansion/improvement	2
Customer focus/surveys/input	3
Internal structure (net)	18
Reorganization/restructuring	7
Team building/staff morale	2
Staffing levels/quality	4
Diversity initiatives	< 1
Rainy day fund/reserves	< 1
Innovation fund	0
Internal communication	2
Contraction/downsizing	3
Leadership (net)	16
Board development/management	4
Leadership development/management training	2
Succession planning/search	1
Change in leadership	7
Greater delegation/participation/change in management style	3
Internal management systems (net)	24
Technology planning/acquisition/use	5
Accounting/financial management	3
Personnel system	2
Staff training/development	2
Formal evaluation	1
Organizational assessment/accreditation processes	3
Outcomes/results management/accountability measures	4
Improved processes/procedures (nonspecific)	4
Other/miscellaneous	3
No answer	4

Q15. Is your organization still working on this particular effort or has your organization completed this effort?

Still working on this effort	75
Completed the effort	23
No response	2

Q16. To date, how many months did your organization work on this effort?

Six months or less	14
Seven months to less than a year	12
One year	15
More than a year to two years	31
More than two years	21
No response	7

Q17. Please indicate how successful the effort was [Q15 = 2] or has been [Q15 = 1] in improving each of the following. Has it been completely successful, mostly successful, somewhat successful, neither successful nor unsuccessful, somewhat unsuccessful, mostly unsuccessful, or completely unsuccessful?

a. Your organizational management

Completely successful	14
Mostly successful	47
Somewhat successful	29
Neither successful nor unsuccessful	7
Somewhat unsuccessful	< 1
Mostly unsuccessful	0
Completely unsuccessful	0
No response	3

b. Your organization's programmatic impact

Completely successful	14
Mostly successful	50
Somewhat successful	25
Neither successful nor unsuccessful	6
Somewhat unsuccessful	1
Mostly unsuccessful	0
Completely unsuccessful	0
No response	4

c. Your organization's overall performance

Completely successful	14
Mostly successful	56
Somewhat successful	18
Neither successful nor unsuccessful	4
Somewhat unsuccessful	1
Mostly unsuccessful	< 1
Completely unsuccessful	0
No response	7

Q18. Which of the following prompted you to undertake this effort to improve your organization's performance? Please check as many as apply.

A crisis or shock to the organization	22
Increasing demand for services	53
Pressure from clients or other stakeholders	24
A particular problem with your organization	30
Availability of funding to work on organizational development	22
Ideas or concerns expressed by your board or staff members	57
Publications or discussions with professional colleagues	20
Other	26
No response to all	3

Q19. In your opinion, did the organization do a great deal of planning before it began this effort to improve its performance, a fair amount of planning, not too much planning, or nearly no planning?

Great deal of planning	25
Fair amount of planning	45
Not too much planning	24
Nearly no planning	4
No response	2

Q20. Roughly how much did this effort cost? If possible, please specify in direct and in-kind costs.

Nothing	17
$5,000 or less	17
$5,001 to $10,000	10
$10,001 to $25,000	8
$25,001 to $50,000	9
More than $50,000	16
No response	23

Q21. Did you have any outside funding to cover this effort?

Yes	30
No	67
No response	3

Q22. Did the funding cover all, most, some, or only a little of the expenses associated with this effort? [Based on those who had outside funding; N = 96.]

All	26
Most	40
Some	30
Only a little	4
No response	0

Q23. Thinking about all the financial resources you had, would you describe them as very adequate, somewhat adequate, not too adequate, or not adequate at all for the performance-building effort?

Very adequate	20
Somewhat adequate	48
Not too adequate	21
Not adequate at all	7
No response	4

Q24. Did you use any of the following resources in this effort to improve the management or programmatic performance of your organization? Please check as many as apply.

Consultants hired for the project	42
Web-based resources	25
Books, manuals, or other written materials	50
Training provided through conferences or workshops	53
Advice from professional colleagues	65
Technical assistance provided by a management support center	16
No response to all	14

Q25. Please describe how helpful each of the following were in the effort to improve your organization's performance. Was it very helpful, somewhat helpful, not too helpful, or not helpful at all?

	Very helpful	Some-what helpful	Not too helpful	Not helpful at all	No response
a. Consultants hired for the project [based on those who used consultants; N = 133]	61	28	8	0	3
b. Web-based resources [based on those who used resources; N = 80]	21	71	5	1	1
c. Books, manuals, or other written materials [based on those who used manuals; N = 159]	28	58	12	0	2
d. Training provided through conferences or workshops [based on those who used training materials; N = 169]	38	54	5	0	2
e. Advice from professional colleagues [based on those who got advice from colleagues; N = 207]	57	38	2	0	2
f. Technical assistance provided by a management support center [based on those who used technical assistance; N = 52]	44	38	10	2	6

Q26. How did you go about selecting a consultant, for example, through a request for proposal, from a list supplied by a funder, to work on this effort to improve your organization's performance? Please describe briefly. [Based on those who sought to improve management or programmatic impact and used consultants. Open ended.]

Q27. Please indicate how much each of the following people were involved in the effort to improve performance. Did this effort involve them a great deal, a fair amount, not too much, or not at all?

	Great deal	Fair amount	Not too much	Not at all	No response
a. The board	31	30	26	8	4
b. Senior staff	79	12	4	1	4
c. Middle management	31	36	11	9	12
d. Frontline staff	28	33	22	9	8

Q28. Who would you say was the strongest advocate, or champion, of the effort?

The board	17
The executive director	57
A senior staff member	6
A department	2
A staff committee	3
The staff as a whole	8
Other	4
No response	3

Q29. Did you involve the people your organization serves such as members or clients directly in this effort to improve your organization's performance?

Yes	51
No	45
No response	4

Q30. Earlier you indicated that this effort was [insert response from Q17c] on your organization's overall performance. Did you primarily base that assessment on a formal evaluation, your own assessment, or objective evidence (for example, new system didn't work) that the effort was [insert response from Q17c]? [Based on those who responded about the success of the effort on the organization's overall performance; N = 296.]

Formal evaluation	11
Your own assessment	57
Objective evidence	29
No response	2

Q31. Please indicate how important each of the following were to the success of your effort to improve organizational performance. [Based on those who said the effort was successful; N = 280 except as noted.]

	Very important	Some-what im-portant	Not too important	Not important at all	No response
a. Board leadership	46	32	15	5	3
b. Adequate time to devote to the effort	61	33	4	< 1	3
c. Adequate funding to devote to the effort	36	38	16	6	3
d. Effective consultants [based on those who had a consultant; N = 120]	53	36	8	3	1
e. Staff commitment	77	16	3	1	4
f. Community support	23	26	30	17	5
g. Events beyond your control	6	7	5	15	68

Q32. Now please indicate how important each of the following were to the lack of success of your effort to improve organizational performance? [Based on those who said the effort was not successful; N = 16 except as noted.]

	Very important	Some-what im-portant	Not too important	Not important at all	No response
a. Lack of board leadership	6	19	13	44	19
b. Inadequate time to devote to the effort	13	31	25	13	19
c. Inadequate funding to devote to the effort	44	6	25	6	19
d. Ineffective consultants [based on those who had a consultant; N = 6]	0	33	0	33	33
e. Lack of staff commitment	13	6	38	25	19
f. Lack of community support	19	6	6	50	19
g. Events beyond your control	19	0	6	0	75

Q33. How likely would you be to engage in another effort to improve the performance of your organization in the future—very likely, somewhat likely, not too likely, or not likely at all?

Very likely	75
Somewhat likely	18
Not too likely	1
Not likely at all	1
No response	5

Q34. Do you strongly agree, somewhat agree, somewhat disagree, or strongly disagree with each of the following statements?

	Strongly agree	Some- what agree	Some- what disagree	Strongly disagree	Not sure/ not appli- cable	No response
a. The work we did to build our organization's performance showed us that change is harder to achieve than we expected.	14	42	27	11	1	5
b. The work we did to build our organization's performance showed us the areas we needed to improve and the areas where we're doing well.	43	41	5	1	3	8
c. The work we did to build our organization's performance showed us that it is very hard to find good consultants.	10	14	20	15	27	14
d. The work we did to build our organization's performance gave us a clearer sense of direction and priorities than we had before.	36	28	5	3	1	28
e. The work we did to build our organization's performance was very stressful for our staff.	10	29	16	10	3	31
f. The work we did to build our organization's performance has led to long-lasting improvements in the organization.	35	23	2	0	4	36

Q35. Thinking specifically about your organization's management and performance, to what extent did this effort improve each of the following? Has it been improved a great deal, somewhat, a little, or not at all?

	A great deal	Some- what	A little	Not at all	No response
a. Morale of management and staff	42	41	8	3	7
b. Your ability to use resources effectively	46	38	6	3	6
c. Your staff's ability to do their job more efficiently	40	38	10	5	7
d. Focus of management	50	35	6	1	8
e. Innovativeness of the organization	40	37	12	3	8
f. Funding of the organization	22	34	20	15	9
g. Client satisfaction	32	36	14	7	10
h. Decisionmaking processes	35	39	11	5	11
i. Accountability among management and staff	41	34	10	3	12
j. Public reputation	36	29	13	6	17

Q36. Are there other outcomes that this effort produced? Please briefly describe them. [Open ended.]

Types of outcomes described were as follows:

External relations (net)	17
Relationships/partnerships/collaborations	2
External communications/marketing/outreach	1
Reputation/public recognition/visibility	7
Greater funding/financial stability	7
Internal structure (net)	15
Expansion/growth/new staff	4
Contraction/exit/staff reductions	1
Change in organizational culture	1
Greater ownership/participation/team orientation	4
Internal communications	1
Morale/pride/satisfaction/retention	4
Leadership (net)	6
Direction/alignment/sense of purpose	4
Board development	2
Leadership development/change	< 1
Internal management systems (net)	7
Efficiency	3
Effectiveness/outcomes	2
General organizational stability/health	1
Staff training	0
Accountability	1
Other (net)	57
Domino effect	1
Clarified SWOTs	3
Created problems/challenges	2
Capacity building still in process	2
No/none	4
Other	2
No answer	43

Q37. Just your best guess, how much did productivity increase due to this effort: less than 10 percent, 10–30 percent, more than 30 percent? [Based on those who said the effort had greatly or somewhat improved the organization's ability to use resources effectively in Q35; N = 269.]

Less than 10 percent	15
10 to 30 percent	54
More than 30 percent	27
No response	4

Q38. Just your best guess, how much did efficiency increase due to this effort: less than 10 percent, 10–30 percent, more than 30 percent? [Based on those who said the effort had greatly or somewhat improved staff's ability to do their job more efficiently in Q35; N = 249.]

Less than 10 percent	12
10 to 30 percent	55
More than 30 percent	27
No response	7

Q39. Approximately how many years has your organization been in operation?

Less than seven years	5
Seven to fifteen years	14
Sixteen to thirty years	31
More than thirty years	42
No response	7

Q40. Approximately how many people work for your organization?

Less than 100	73
100–999	18
1,000–9,999	3
10,000–49,999	1
50,000 or more	0
No response	6

Q41. Which of these categories best describes the size of your organization's annual budget?

Less than $500,000	19
$500,000 to less than $1 million	21
$1 million to less than $2 million	12
$2 million to less than $10 million	26
$10 million to less than $50 million	10
$50 million to less than $100 million	2
$100 million to less than $500 million	2
$500 million to less than $1 billion	0
$1 billion to less than $50 billion	< 1
More than $50 billion	0
No response	7

Demographic questions

D1. Respondent's sex

Male	47
Female	47
No response	6

D2. What is your age?

Eighteen to twenty-nine	1
Thirty to forty-four	18
Forty-five to fifty-four	40
Fifty-five to sixty-four	29
Sixty-five or older	6
No response	7

D3. What is the highest level of education you have completed?

High school	1
Some college	9
College graduate	32
Master's degree	39
Ph.D.	7
Other professional degree	6
No response	7

D4. Are you of Hispanic origin or descent, such as Mexican, Puerto Rican, Cuban, or some other Latino background?

Yes	2
No	88
Don't know	0
Prefer not to answer	4
Refuse to answer	6

D5. What is your race? White, African American or black, Asian, or some other race? [If Hispanic/Latino (D4 = 1) ask:] Are you white Latino, black Latino, or some other race?

White/white Latino	85
Black or African American/black Latino	2
Asian	< 1
Other	1
Don't know	0
Prefer not to answer	5
Refuse to answer	6

Appendix B

Capacity Building in Low-Income-Serving Children and Family Organizations

Human service organizations have some of the toughest missions in the nonprofit sector. They provide child care for low-income working parents, run after-school programs that build self-esteem, protect children from neglect, provide alternatives for troubled juveniles, and guide the journey for low-income families from welfare to work. In many ways, these nonprofits are America's other first responders. They often answer the first call for help from America's most vulnerable citizens and make some of the most difficult choices in society.

In an effort to better understand the organizational needs of these nonprofits, the Annie E. Casey Foundation provided additional funding to expand the final sample of low-income-serving children and family nonprofits by eighty-five, thereby increasing the total sample of nonprofits to 403. Of the 403, 125 met the two basic criteria to be defined as low-income-serving children and family organizations: (1) respondents said that the words "low income" described the people their organization served very well, and (2) they also said the same about the words "children and/or families." Of the 278 organizations that did not meet this strict test, sixty-two said that the words "low income" described the people their organization served very well, while 107 said the same of "children and/or families." They simply did not meet both tests.

The central purpose of this brief appendix is to ask whether and how low-income-serving children and family nonprofits differ from other nonprofits in their capacity-building activities and success. In a sentence, these organizations shared many organizational characteristics with the rest of the sample, suggesting that capacity building is one of the ties that bind different parts of the sector; however, the respondents reported greater growth in programs and services but lower levels of overall capacity-building success:

—36 percent of respondents at the low-income-serving children and family organizations reported a great deal of growth in their programs and services over five years preceding the survey, while 39 percent reported a great deal of growth in the number of clients, compared with 25 and 33 percent of their peers, respectively.

—31 percent of the respondents at the low-income-serving children and family organizations reported that their organization's capacity-building effort was somewhat successful or less in improving overall performance, compared with 24 percent of their colleagues.

—The respondents at the low-income-serving children and family organizations were also more likely to report that their organization's effort showed them that change is harder to achieve than they expected and that the effort was stressful for their staff.

If the question is what might explain the lower rates of success, the answer is not in the organizational history of capacity building. Indeed, the 125 low-income-serving children and family nonprofits were just as likely as their 278 peers to have engaged in all four areas of organizational improvement: 59 percent of respondents in the first group said their organization had engaged all four areas, compared with 58 percent of the second group.

However, when given a list of specific interventions, the 125 organizations were much more likely to report that they had engaged in collaboration (93 versus 94 percent), team building (83 versus 71 percent), recruitment of a more diverse staff (38 versus 23 percent), board development (84 versus 76 percent), leadership development (73 versus 59 percent), new accounting systems (71 versus 58 percent), evaluation (65 versus 59 percent), organizational assessment (60 versus 47 percent), and outcomes measurement (47 versus 42 percent). Except for media relations, where they trailed their peers 54 to 63 percent, the low-income-serving children and family organizations had done more work than other nonprofits trying to build the scaffolding of successful organizational improvement.

Indeed, of the twenty-three specific interventions listed, 30 percent of the low-income-serving children and family organizations had done more than fifteen, compared with 19 percent of their peers. If these organizations were performing poorly, it was certainly not for lack of trying. Unfortunately, as noted in the body of the book, we cannot know whether these efforts succeeded. There was simply not enough time in the survey to ask questions about every possible past intervention.

The low-income-serving children and family organizations also differed from their peers in both what they did and how they did it. First, comparing the 125 and 278 specific capacity-building efforts, respondents from the low-income-serving children and family organizations were less likely to report that their organization had tried to improve external relationships and more likely to focus on internal systems. Thus 34 percent of the low-income-serving children and family organizations focused on internal systems, while 28 percent focused on external relationships (compared with 26 and 33 percent of their peers, respectively).

Whatever the focus, improvement efforts in the low-income-serving children and family organizations were more likely to have been launched for different reasons. Thus 56 percent of 125 efforts were prompted by increasing demand for services and 31 percent by available funding, compared with 51 and 21 percent, respectively, among the group of 278 efforts. In contrast, 21 percent of the 278 efforts were launched because of publications or discussions with professional colleagues, compared with just 13 percent of the 125 efforts.

Although the two groups of nonprofits did not differ greatly on the amount of planning, the cost of the effort, the extent to which the effort had been completed at the time of the survey, the use of hard evidence, and the level of board, senior staff, middle management, frontline, or community involvement, respondents from the low-income-serving children and family organizations were more likely to report that their effort involved outside funding and much greater contact with the outside world. In other words, the low-income-serving children and family organizations followed the standard capacity-building practices of their peers and had several clear advantages. On the one hand, for example,

71 percent of the 125 efforts involved a great deal or a fair amount of planning, compared with 70 percent of the 278, while 49 percent of the 125 efforts cost $10,000 or less, compared with 44 percent of the 278. Moreover, 34 percent of the 125 efforts involved at least some outside funding, compared with 28 percent of the 278.

On the other hand, 49 percent of the 125 efforts lasted less than a year, compared with 40 percent of the 278, while 36 percent of the 125 efforts were rated as having inadequate financial resources, compared with 26 percent of the 278. The low-income-serving children and family organizations may have followed standard practices in general, but they clearly operated under a tighter time frame and with less financial support.

Despite these negatives, the 125 organizations reported somewhat greater success on several key capacity-building outputs and outcomes. They were more likely, for example, to say that their organization's effort produced a great deal of impact on staff morale and innovation and much more likely to report efficiency and productivity gains.

The question, therefore, is why the 125 respondents would rate their efforts as less successful overall. Further statistical analysis using the same measures described in chapter 3 provides at least some evidence of the pattern. As with the 318 efforts chronicled in the book, how respondents judged an effort's success in improving organizational management and programmatic impacts was by far the most significant predictor of over-all impact on organizational performance. Indeed, these two measures were the only significant predictors in the head-to-head comparison among the 125 low-income-serving children and family organizations and were the top two of just three significant predictors among the 278 peers.

However, when these two measures are removed from the analysis, a different picture emerges. For the 125 organizations, having adequate funding was the top predictor of success, while the use of soft evidence came in second as a negative factor. For the 278 organizations, the use of hard evidence was the top predictor of success, followed by adequate funding and a deeper history of capacity building.

Despite all the advantages that the low-income-serving children and family organizations have going into the capacity-building process, they face two obvious obstacles to achieving success. First, as I have argued elsewhere in research funded by the Annie E. Casey Foundation, these organizations are in desperate need of repair.[1] Even a cascade of success-ful capacity-building efforts might not make a dent in their deep improvement agendas. Second, because of time, resource, and caseload pressures, many of their capacity-building efforts are underimplemented or quickly lost in a high-turnover work force. Most low-income-serving children and family organizations are so clearly stuck in the enterprising stage of organizational development that they cannot take a breath. Besieged by increasing demand, facing deep cuts in their budget, and facing serious staffing pressures, the organizations have little opportunity for past experience to make a difference in current practice; even the gains in morale, innovation, and productivity are washed away as these organizations struggle with some of the toughest missions in the sector.

Notes

Chapter One

1. Claire Gaudiani, "Sustaining America's Tradition of Generosity," *Chronicle of Philanthropy*, October 2, 2003; Jeffrey Berry, "Nonprofit Groups Shouldn't Be Afraid to Lobby," *Chronicle of Philanthropy*, November 27, 2003; Lester Salamon, "Nonprofit World Faces Many Dangers," *Chronicle of Philanthropy*, January 8, 2004; William Schambra, "The New Politics of Philanthropy," *Chronicle of Philanthropy*, November 13, 2003; Pablo Eisenberg, "What Congress Can Do to Fight Charity and Foundation Abuses," *Chronicle of Philanthropy*, March 18, 2004.

2. For an insightful discussion of the impact of state budgets on nonprofits and the impact of economic recession on the nonprofit sector, see Wood Bowman, "Fiscal Crisis in the States: Its Impact on Nonprofit Organizations and the People They Serve" (Washington: Aspen Institute, Nonprofit Sector Research Fund, November 18, 2003).

3. The survey of 770 randomly selected Americans was conducted by Princeton Survey Research Associates on behalf of the Center for Public Service on October 2–12, 2003.

4. Bill Bradley, Paul Jansen, and Les Silverman, "The Nonprofit Sector's $100 Billion Opportunity," *Harvard Business Review* (May 2003), reprint R0305G, p. 1.

5. Lester Salamon, "Charities Shouldn't Be Urged to Act Like Enron," *Chronicle of Philanthropy*, May 29, 2003.

6. Alison Fine, "Letter to the Editor," *Chronicle of Philanthropy*, August 7, 2003 (www.philanthropy.com [accessed on March 3, 2004]).

7. Robert Egger with Howard Yoon, *Begging for Change: The Dollars and Sense of Making Nonprofits Responsive, Efficient, and Rewarding for All* (HarperBusiness, 2004).

8. Paul C. Light, *Making Nonprofits Work* (Brookings, 2000); Paul C. Light, *Pathways to Nonprofit Excellence* (Brookings, 2002).

9. Paul C. Light, *Monitoring Government: Federal Inspectors General and the Search for Accountability* (Brookings, 1993).

Chapter Two

1. The list can be found in Paul C. Light, *Government's Greatest Achievements: From Civil Rights to Homeland Security* (Brookings, 2002).

2. See Paul C. Light, "Nonprofit-Like: Tongue-Twister or Aspiration," *Nonprofit Quarterly,* vol. 8, no. 2 (Summer 2001), available at www.tsne.org/print/87.html [May 7, 2004].

3. The survey of the nonprofit work force was conducted from October 29, 2001, to January 2, 2002, and involved a random sample of 1,140 employees; the survey of federal employees was conducted from February 7 to June 1, 2001, and involved 1,051 employees; and the survey of private sector employees was conducted from May 11, 2001, to January 22, 2002, and involved 1,005 employees. The 1,140 nonprofit employees were reached through random-digit telephone dialing, conducted under the direction of Princeton Survey Research Associates. The interviews averaged twenty-seven minutes in length, and interviewers made up to twenty calls to each sampled respondent in an attempt to complete the interview. The sample was randomly drawn to ensure representation of all nonprofit employees. Although it is not an exact census, it does reveal the general demographic shape of the sector. Demographic patterns might vary substantially across subsectors such as community-based organizations, child care agencies, think tanks, hospitals, and so forth. The response rate for the overall survey was 71 percent. For results based on the total sample, one can say with 95 percent confidence that the error attributable to sampling and other random effects was within approximately plus or minus 3 percentage points. In addition to sampling error, wording of the question and practical difficulties in conducting telephone surveys could introduce error or bias into the findings of this survey. By sex, 32 percent of the sample was male, 68 percent female. By age, 11 percent of the sample was eighteen to twenty-nine years of age, 13 percent was thirty to thirty-nine years of age, 33 percent was forty to forty-nine years of age, and 32 percent was fifty years of age or older. By race-ethnicity, 84 percent of the sample was white, 7 percent African American, 4 percent Latino or Hispanic, 3 percent other, and 1 percent Asian or Pacific Islander. By organizational mission, 33 percent of the sample worked in health, 39 percent in education, 25 percent in social services, 7 percent in economic or community development, 2 percent in arts, 2 percent in science, and 1 percent in environmental organizations. By age, 4 percent of the sample worked in organizations that were less than seven years old, 8 percent worked in organizations seven to fifteen years old, 18 percent worked in organizations fifteen to thirty years old, and 70 percent worked in organizations more than thirty years old. By scope, 79 percent of the sample worked in a local organization, 11 percent worked in a national organization, and 8 percent worked in an international organization.

4. This question was only asked of nonprofit employees.

5. Larger, older organizations are defined in the analysis underpinning this paragraph as organizations more than thirty years old and with more than 150 employees, while smaller, younger organizations are defined as less than thirty years old and with fewer than seventy-five employees.

6. The sample size was 208 for organizations with less than seventy-five employees and less than thirty years old, and 536 for organizations with more than seventy-five employees and more than thirty years old.

7. Lester Salamon, "Nonprofit World Faces Many Dangers," *Chronicle of Philanthropy,* January 8, 2004.

8. Paul C. Light, *Pathways to Nonprofit Excellence* (Brookings, 2002).

9. There is a healthy debate in the research literature about whether and when to trust employee judgments. Recent evidence suggests that there may be good reason to trust the retrospective judgments of respondents. This literature is particularly important for readers who worry about the validity of the assessments of capacity-building success used later in this book. See C. Chet Miller, Laura B. Cardinal, and William H. Glick, "Retrospective Reports in Organizational Research: A Reexamination of Recent Evidence," *Academy of Management Journal*, vol. 40, no. 1 (1997), pp. 189–204.

10. The summing creates more variation against which to measure the predictive power of the measures of organizational capacity.

11. This conclusion was produced through ordinary least-squares regression of trust in one's own organization to do the right thing. The four predictors are all significant predictors. Strength is measured using standardized beta weights, and significance is based on t tests, which indicate the chance that a given result is not the result of random occurrence. The adjusted R^2 for the overall model is 0.336, which means that the analysis explains roughly 34 percent of the variation in employee views of overall effectiveness, which is significant at the 0.000 level. The table only includes explanations that were significant at the 0.05 level or greater, which means one can have 95 percent confidence that the explanations outlined in box 2-1 and table 2-1 are statistically significant predictors of organizational effectiveness.

12. See Lester Salamon, *The State of Nonprofit America* (Brookings, 2002).

13. This section draws heavily on Paul C. Light, "To Give or Not to Give: The Crisis in Confidence in Charities," Reform Watch Brief 7 (Brookings, December 2003); the July 2001 survey was conducted by Independent Sector, while the rest were conducted by Brookings.

14. The actual wording of the question was, "How much confidence do you have in charitable organizations—a lot, some, or none at all?" For grammatical ease, I use the term "nonprofits" to mean "charitable organizations" in this section of the analysis. The samples for all public opinion surveys of the Center for Public Service were collected through random-digit dialing, and the surveys were conducted by telephone. Potential respondents were contacted at least ten times before they were dropped from the sample.

15. See Paul C. Light and Judith M. Labiner, "A Vote of Renewed Confidence: How Americans View Presidential Appointees and Government in the Wake of the September 11 Terrorist Attacks" (Washington: Presidential Appointee Initiative, October 18, 2001).

16. Robert D. Putnam, "Bowling Together," *American Prospect*, vol. 13, no. 3 (February 11, 2002), available at www.prospect.org/print-friendly/pring/v13/3/putnam-r.html [March 9, 2004].

17. Ben Gose, "42% of Americans Say Relief Effort Damaged Faith in Nonprofit Groups," *Chronicle of Philanthropy*, August 15, 2002.

18. Independent Sector, *Keeping the Trust: Confidence in Charitable Organizations in an Age of Scrutiny* (Washington, 2002).

19. Independent Sector, *Keeping the Trust*.

20. Lester Salamon, "Nonprofit World Faces Many Dangers," *Chronicle of Philanthropy*, January 8, 2004.

21. United Way of America, *Impact Matters: The Essential Attributes of a Community Impact United Way* (Alexandria, Va., 2003), pp. 6–7.

22. These results were produced through ordinary least-squares regression of confidence in nonprofits in the October 2003 survey. Strength is measured using standardized beta weights; significance is based on t tests, which indicate the chance that a given result is not the result of random occurrence. The adjusted R^2 for the discretionary giving model is 0.133, meaning that the analysis explains roughly 13 percent of the variation in giving, a modest result that is significant at the 0.000 level. The adjusted R^2 for the discretionary

volunteering model is 0.082, meaning that the analysis explains roughly 8 percent of the variation in volunteering, a modest result that is nonetheless significant at the 0.000 level. The relatively low R^2 reflects the fact that the dependent variables—discretionary giving and volunteering—come from simple yes-no questions; that is, respondents were only asked whether they had given any money or volunteered, not how much money or time.

Chapter Three

1. This inventory comes from Pierre Mourier and Martin Smith, *Conquering Organizational Change* (Atlanta: Center for Effective Performance, 2001).

2. The first four studies on the list come from Mourier and Smith, *Conquering Organizational Change*; the fifth comes from Edward H. Bowman, Harbir Singh, Michael Useem, and Raja Bhadury, "When Does Restructuring Improve Economic Performance?" *California Management Review*, vol. 41, no. 2 (1999), p. 48; and the sixth comes from Jennifer A. LaClair and Ravi P. Rao, "Helping Employees Embrace Change," *McKinsey Quarterly*, vol. 4 (2002), pp. 17–20.

3. Darrell Rigby, *The Bottom Line on Management* (New York: Bain and Company, 2003), p. 2.

4. Barbara Blumenthal, *Investing in Capacity Building: A Guide to High-Impact Approaches* (New York: Foundation Center, 2003), p. 4.

5. Daniel P. Forbes, "Measuring the Unmeasurable: Empirical Studies of Nonprofit Organizational Effectiveness from 1977 to 1997," *Nonprofit and Voluntary Sector Quarterly*, vol. 127, no. 2 (June 1998), p. 198. Forbes did his research as a graduate student at the Stern School of Business at New York University, and he continues his work as an assistant professor at the Carlson School of Business at the University of Minnesota.

6. For a defense of the Internal Revenue Service Form 990 reports, see Linda M. Lampkin and Elizabeth T. Boris, "Nonprofit Organization Data," *American Behavioral Scientist*, vol. 45, no. 11 (July 2003), pp. 1675–718. The authors have been deeply involved in improving the Internal Revenue Service data and in making them more accessible to scholars.

7. Jennifer A. Lammers, "Know Your Ratios? Everyone Else Does," *Nonprofit Quarterly*, vol. 10, no. 1 (Spring 2003), p. 1.

8. Cassandra Benjamin, *Broken Yardstick: Administrative Cost Rates as a Measure of Nonprofit Effectiveness* (San Francisco: CompassPoint, 2000), p. 12.

9. Clara Miller, "The Looking-Glass World of Nonprofit Money: Managing in For-Profit's Shadow Universe," *Nonprofit Quarterly* (forthcoming, 2004).

10. Mark A. Hager, "Public Trust in the Public Face of Charities," *Democracy and Society*, vol. 1 (Spring 2004), p. 15.

11. See McKinsey and Company, *Effective Capacity Building in Nonprofits* (Washington: Venture Philanthropy Partners, 2001); Roberts Enterprise Development Fund, *Analyzing the Value of Social Purpose Enterprise within a Social Return on Investment Framework* (San Francisco, 2001).

12. For a summary of the disputes, see Paul C. Light, *The Robust Organization* (forthcoming, 2004).

13. See Erik Brynjolfsson, "The Productivity Paradox of Information Technology," *Communication of the ACM*, vol. 36, no. 12 (December 1993), pp. 67–77; Erik Brynjolfsson and Loren Hitt, "Is Information Technology Spending Productive? New Evidence and New Results," paper presented at International Conference on Information Systems, Orlando, Fla., 1993; and Anandhi Bharadwaj, Sundar Bharadwaj, and Benn R. Konsynski, "Information Technology Effects on Firm Performance as Measures by Tobin's q," *Management Science*, vol. 45, no. 7 (1999), pp. 1010–23.

14. Charles Corbett, Maria Montes, and David Kirsch, "The Financial Impact of ISO 9000 Certification: An Empirical Analysis," unpublished paper (Anderson School, University of California, Los Angeles; Universidad Carlos III; and University of Maryland, June 1, 2000); see also James Treece, "U.S. Reporting Standards Cut Toyota Profits," *Automotive News*, vol. 76, no. 5998 (January 7, 2002), p. 1.

15. This financial threshold was designed to increase the probability that respondent organizations would have at least one capacity-building effort to describe in detail, the notion being that very small nonprofits are far less likely to engage in capacity building.

16. This survey was conducted in November 2003 by Elizabeth Hubbard and showed the following: First, of the 150 nonrespondents, roughly a fifth, or thirty-three, were either (a) in the midst of an executive transition, which meant that no one could participate in the follow-up survey, or (b) worked in foundations, endowments, or volunteer organizations that were ineligible for the survey. Second, of the respondents in the 117 organizations that were eligible and did exist, twenty-nine did not return the phone calls inviting them to participate in the follow-up survey, refused to participate once they were reached, or were in the midst of an executive transition and had no one to participate. Third, of the eighty-eight respondents who did participate in the nonresponse survey, thirty-four simply did not remember receiving the original request or three follow-ups, and eleven refused to answer the question about why they did not respond. Fourth, of the forty-three respondents who did remember the survey and did answer the nonresponse question, sixteen said they did not have time to participate, seven said they worked in an organization that had a policy against participating in surveys, two actually remembered doing the survey, one said the website did not work, and the rest gave a personal or otherwise vague answer.

17. Of the 117 eligible respondents in the survey of nonrespondents, seventy-six, or 65 percent, said their organization was doing something to improve performance.

18. The eighteen follow-up interviews referenced here and below were conducted in November and December 2003 and lasted between thirty minutes and an hour. The interviews were tape recorded and transcribed for accuracy. Respondents were promised confidentiality in return for candor.

19. Peter Frumkin and Mark T. Kim, "Strategic Positioning and the Financing of Nonprofit Organizations," *Public Administration Review*, vol. 61, no. 3 (2001), pp. 273–374.

20. Elizabeth Hubbard is based in Columbus, Ohio, and participated in all aspects of the capacity-building project, as did her colleague Lisa Zellmer, who is based in Minneapolis, Minnesota.

21. Richard L. Daft, "A Dual-Core Model of Organizational Innovation," *Academy of Management Journal*, vol. 21, no. 2 (1978), p. 195.

22. Christine W. Letts, William Ryan, and Allen Grossman, "Virtuous Capital: What Foundations Can Learn from Venture Capitalists," *Harvard Business Review* (March–April 1997), reprint 97207, p. 7.

Chapter Four

1. McKinsey and Company, *Effective Capacity Building in Nonprofit Organizations* (Washington: Venture Philanthropy Partners, 2001).

2. These responses come from Q35 in the survey, which invited respondents to briefly describe any other outcomes that their organization's effort produced.

3. See Paul C. Light, *The Robust Organization* (forthcoming, 2004).

4. Paul C. Light, *Pathways to Nonprofit Excellence* (Brookings, 2002), p. 37.

5. The rest of respondents did not describe their improvement effort in detail.

6. I am grateful to students in my Designing Organizational Change seminar at New York University for helping me to develop this list of explanations.

7. See, for example, Diane Baillargeon, Dennis Smith, and Gabrielle Gerhard, "Lessons from the DeWitt Wallace–Reader's Digest Management Initiative for Organizations That Serve Youth," unpublished report (1995).

8. See table 4-6 for the data.

Chapter Five

1. Clara Miller, "The Looking-Glass World of Nonprofit Money: Managing in For-Profit's Shadow Universe," *Nonprofit Quarterly* (forthcoming).

2. Robert E. Cole, "Learning from the Quality Movement: What Did and Didn't Happen and Why?" *California Management Review*, vol. 41, no. 1 (1998), p. 63.

3. Paul J. DiMaggio, Janet A. Weiss, and Charles T. Clotfelter, "Data to Support Scholarship on Nonprofit Organizations," *American Behavioral Scientist*, vol. 45, no. 11 (July 2002), pp. 1620–41.

4. The survey was conducted by Princeton Survey Research Associates on behalf of the Center for Public Service from March 24 to April 23, 2003, and involved 1,002 about-to-graduate majors in liberal arts, social sciences, social work, and education.

5. Active Community Unit, *Voluntary and Community Sector Infrastructure* (London: Home Office, September 2003), p. i.

Chapter Six

1. Lisa Zellmer organized, scheduled, and facilitated the site visits on my behalf. She also participated in all aspects of the site visits and subsequent data analysis on which this chapter is based.

2. All of the site visit interviews were tape recorded and transcribed. Individuals were promised confidentiality in return for candor.

3. Paul C. Light, *The Robust Organization* (forthcoming, 2004).

4. See Andrew H. van de Ven and Marshall Scott Poole, "Explaining Development and Change in Organizations," *Academy of Management Journal*, vol. 20, no. 3 (1995), pp. 510–40, for an introduction to the various theories—or "motors"—that are used to explain organizational development and change.

5. This survey can be found in the appendixes of Paul C. Light, *Pathways to Nonprofit Excellence* (Brookings, 2002). The twenty-five organizations discussed here were selected from the 250 high-performing organizations interviewed for the *Pathways* project.

6. See the change at www.care.org.

Appendix B

1. Paul C. Light, *The Health of the Human Services Workforce* (Washington: Center for Public Service, 2003).

Index